Infantry
Weapons
of the World.

Christopher F. Foss
and T. J. Gander.

Charles Scribner's Sons
NEW YORK

Addenda

The new Soviet rifle mentioned in the Introduction has now been identified as the AKS-74 with a calibre of 5.45mm. The rifle is a development of the AKM and fires conventional ammunition, which is contained in a plastic magazine. A small muzzle brake is fitted, and the overall appearance is that of a AKM — a wooden butt is fitted.

The authors would like to acknowledge the help of Parker-Hale (Great Britain).

Contents

Copyright © Christopher F. Foss & T. J. Gander 1979

Copyright under the Berne Convention

All rights reserved. No part of this book
may be reproduced in any form without the
permission of Charles Scribner's Sons

1 3 5 7 9 11 13 15 17 19 I/C 20 18 16 14 12 10 8 6 4 2

Printed in Great Britain

Library of Congress Catalog Card Number 79-53487
ISBN 0-684-16246-6

Introduction

The second edition of *Infantry Weapons of the World* follows the same format of the first edition in that it covers all the main infantry weapons in service around the world, along with a selection of weapons that are still under development. Like the first edition, mortars above 60mm are not included as they are covered by the companion *Artillery of the World*, along with other heavy infantry weapons such as the large recoilless weapons. Anti-tank missiles are likewise covered in *Missiles of the World*, another Ian Allan companion book.

When the first edition was being written the calibre and ammunition field within NATO and Allied nations was far from settled. Then, as now, both 7.62mm and 5.56mm were in front-line service with older calibres such as 7.92mm still to be found in many armouries, along with a whole host of weapon types and models. Today the standardisation scene is no less cluttered and indeed has grown worse as the NATO trials to determine a new service round continue. These trials centre on the need for a centralised and rationalised ammunition supply for NATO and consequently a large number of other nations. Nearly every NATO nation has entered its own ammunition design along with new weapons to fire it, but already with the trials far from complete, the usual political problems have made themselves apparent. At the time of writing the West German 4.7mm round with its combustible propellant case has proved to be too advanced a concept for service use but the West Germans seem determined to continue its development whatever the outcome of the competition. To date the favourite seems to be the American improved 5.56mm round but the final result of the competition will not be made known for some time yet and by that time each nation may once more have gone its own way, thus nullifying the whole concept of the project.

Although the latest Soviet infantry rifle has not yet been seen publicly, news of it is now filtering through to the West. By the few rumours that are current at the time of writing this new rifle uses a calibre of around 5.56mm with a caseless propellant. Electrical ignition is used with the batteries for this purpose being carried in pouches strapped to the user's chest. This departure to a smaller calibre by the Eastern Bloc is understandable and is made all the easier by the fact that their ammunition plants have to turn out only one calibre and very few types of round — even weapon standardisation throughout the armies of the Warsaw Pact is becoming a distinct possibility, despite slight variations from state to state. A valuable adjunct to this weapon standardisation is the general quality of Soviet weapons themselves. Designed for ease of manufacture and ruggedly built, the latest generation of Soviet infantry weapons have a general simplicity and ease of use that is usually absent in many Western designs — the Soviet PK machine gun family is a case in point — and what is perhaps more important is that they are already in service at a time when comparable Western designs are still under development.

But the Soviet Bloc do not have a monopoly of good weapon design. The Israeli Galil has now had its first operational testing, and the Soviet Bloc still does not have anything to compare with the American 40mm grenade launchers. Numerous American design concepts such as the various machine gun projects show considerable promise, and it must not be forgotten that the British 4.85mm Individual Weapon, at present undergoing the NATO ammunition trials, seems likely to have a long future ahead. The use of optical sights on the latter is a reminder that SUIT and other reflex optical systems may soon replace the time-honoured iron sights.

But despite all these new models and numerous innovations the infantry of the world often carry rifles, pistols and other weapons that were once used by their fathers and their grandfathers. Elderly rifles and sub-machine guns still occupy the armoury racks of many nations, not always for front-line use but for use by the various second-line and para-military formations formed by most nations. The same weapons keep turning up in the hands of those concerned in the various types of civil and anti-establishment conflicts that continue to disturb the peace of the world, so their inclusion is once more necessary but unfortunately it has not proved possible to mention every type likely to be encountered. The recent fighting in the Lebanon was conducted by combatants using weapons from around the world and of all ages from German World War II MG34s to American Springfield rifles and Soviet AK-47s. Also noticed were Mauser rifles from numerous sources, Thompson sub-machine guns and Czech ZB vz37 machine guns. This book is unable to mention them all.

As always, the authors are grateful to the many governments, manufacturers and individuals who have helped in compiling this book, and especially due for our thanks are the ever-helpful staff of the Pattern Room at Enfield.

Additional material and photographs would be welcomed by the authors, and any such material should be forwarded to *Infantry Weapons of the World*, Ian Allan Limited, Terminal House, Shepperton TW17 8AS, England.

Christopher F. Foss
T. J. Gander

Abbreviations

Acknowledgements

The authors would like to thank the following companies and individuals for their most valuable assistance in the preparation of this book.

Aerojet Ordnance and Manufacturing Company USA
Airborne Forces Museum (Aldershot, England)
American Research and Development Co
Argentine Ministry of Defence
Armalite Incorporated (USA)
Australian Army
Austrian Army
Beretta (Italy)
Breda (Italy)
Carl Walther (Germany)
CETME (Spain)
Colt Industries (USA)
Esperanza Company (Spain)
FFV (Sweden)
Finnish Army
FN (Belgium)
French Army
General Dynamics (Pomona Division)
German Army
Heckler and Koch GmbH (Germany)
Israel Military Industries
MBB (Germany)
Ministry of Defence (Army), United Kingdom
Norwegian Army
Rheinmetall GmbH (Germany)
Soltam Limited (Israel)
Sterling Armament Company (Great Britain)
Steyr-Daimler-Puch AG (Austria)
Sturm, Ruger and Company Incorporated (USA)
Swiss Industrial Group
Thomson-Brandt (France)
United Kingdom Land Forces
United States Army
United States Marine Corps
Valmet (Finland)

Glossary

Ammunition Term for the complete round needed to fire a gun.

Automatic A weapon that will fire, reload and fire until prevented from doing so by an external mechanism. Often used to describe a semi-automatic pistol.

Barrel A steel tube in a gun along which the bullet is fired.

Bolt A metal device that holds the round in the chamber ready for firing. May be mechanically or physically locked or free to move as in a blowback mechanism.

Blowback General term used to describe the action of many automatic weapons when an unlocked bolt is returned to the rear by the explosion of the cartridge propellant. Locking is usually effected by the mass of the breechblock.

Breech Rear face of the barrel.

Breechblock Part of an action that holds or locks the round into the chamber for firing and moves back for ejection of the spent cartridge and loading of the next round.

Bullet The projectile fired from a small-arm.

Butt/Butt stock On a shoulder arm the part of the weapon against the firer's shoulder. On a hand gun the part of the gun held in the hand.

4

Calibre/Caliber Internal dimension of the barrel measured from land to land.

Carbine Short rifle.

Cartridge A complete round of fixed ammunition.

Chamber Part of the barrel that holds the cartridge ready for firing.

Change lever Lever usually near the trigger that selects mode of fire. Usually has three positions — automatic, single shot, safe. Sometimes called selector lever or catch.

Cocking The action of mechanically or manually preparing a weapon's mechanism ready for firing.

Cocking handle The handle or lever used to cock a weapon.

Compensator A muzzle attachment used to direct some portion of the gases escaping from the muzzle upwards to counteract a weapon's tendency to rise when fired.

Cylinder The part of a revolver used to hold rounds ready for firing.

Ejector Part of a gun mechanism that forces the spent cartridge case out of the gun. Usually a fixed projection.

Extractor Part of a gun mechanism, usually on a bolt or breechblock that withdraws the cartridge case from the chamber.

Firing pin Part of the firing mechanism that actually strikes the primer to fire the gun. May be fixed or mechanically operated, and is usually on the bolt, breechblock or frame.

Flash hider Device fixed to the muzzle to hide the flash produced when firing. Sometimes known as a flash suppressor.

Frame Part of a revolver that carries the cylinder and barrel. May be fixed or hinged.

Hammer Swinging part of a firing mechanism which may hit the primer for firing, or deliver the force via a firing pin. Usually fitted to revolvers, and may be internal or external.

Handgun Term used to denote a firearm that can be held in one hand.

Jacket Metal covering of a bullet.

Kick Recoil forces felt by the firer of a weapon.

Land Raised portion of rifling.

Magazine Device used on small arms to hold rounds ready for loading and firing. May be either box type or drum.

Mainspring Internal spring used to drive forward a bolt or breechblock.

Muzzle velocity Speed of a bullet as it leaves the muzzle. Sometimes referred to as V_0.

Pistol Term used to signify a handgun in which the chamber is permanently aligned with the barrel. This includes revolvers and some automatic pistols but the term is now used to cover any form of handgun.

Primer A small charge in the base of a cartridge which fires the main propellant. On most small arms this is done mechanically but some weapons use electricity.

Propellant The charge inside a cartridge that propels the bullet.

Range The distance to which a bullet can be fired. Usually defined as maximum practical which is the range at which the bullet will still have a useful striking power.

Rate of fire Number of rounds fired per minute. The *Cyclic* rate is that possible in one minute if an uninterrupted supply of ammunition is maintained. The *practical* rate includes the time lost for changing magazines, etc.

Receiver Part of weapon containing the bolt/breechblock and mainspring, sometimes known as the body.

Revolver Type of handgun that holds available rounds in a cylinder.

Rifle General term used to denote a small-arm with a long rifled barrel that usually fires single shots only.

Rifling Grooves cut inside a barrel to impart stabilising spin to a bullet.

Round General term used to denote cartridge.

Safety/Safety catch Mechanical or manually applied device to prevent a weapon firing.

Sear Lever between the trigger and firing pin or hammer to give controlled leverage to firing mechanism.

Semi-automatic Term applied to small-arm that fires once, ejects spent case reloads but does not fire again until the trigger is pressed.

Sidearm Small-arms that can be carried on a belt and fired from one hand. Was used to denote pistols only but now also includes small sub-machine guns.

Sights Devices used to aim a weapon accurately. Divided into fore and rear sights. The foresight is usually a fixed metal post or spline, while the rear sight is usually at the rear of the weapon and may incorporate many refinements such as a ramp or rising frame to accommodate increases in range and wind velocity. The simplest rearsight on a pistol is usually a simple notch to be aligned with the foresight. Some weapons use telescopic or other optical sights. A flipsight is a folding rear-sight which can be 'flipped up' for use.

Singlepoint A new form of weapon sight that projects a white spot in a tube over a small-arm to visual infinity. Aligning the white spot (while both the firer's eyes are open) will accurately aim the weapon.

Slide An external breechblock, usually found on semi-automatic pistols.

Small-arm General term that is usually used to refer to a weapon that can be carried by one man.

Stock Part of a small-arm held by the firer and used to aim the weapon. Usually of wood but plastic and metal are now often used.

Sub-machine gun Automatic weapon, firing pistol ammunition, with a short barrel carried and used by one man.

Trigger Lever operated manually to fire a weapon.

Addendum

The NATO Small-Arms Trials

At the time of going to press more information is available as to the progress of the NATO trials taking place in West Germany as part of the programme to determine a new standard infantry calibre. It now seems certain that some form of improved 5.56mm cartridge will eventually emerge as the eventual 'winner', but it also seems certain that no one rifle or weapon will emerge as an overall standard NATO firearm. The weapons taking part in the trials are as follows:

France FAMAS Type 3. This is the latest version of the MAS automatic rifle which fires a normal 5.56mm cartridge.

Belgium Belgium has entered two weapons, an automatic rifle and the Minimi light support weapon, both firing the improved S109 5.56mm rounds. While the Belgian round uses a different rifling this is not thought to be a long-term disadvantage when compared with the American 5.56mm round. However, the Belgian round does have a heavier bullet with a steel core which has proved to be difficult to mass produce and still retain a fair measure of ballistic stability. The automatic rifle used in the trials is an improved version of the FN CAL.

United Kingdom While the British 4.85mm cartridge is seen to have many ballistic advantages over the current 5.56mm round it is now acknowledged to have little chance of eventual adoption on the grounds of incompatibility with existing ammunition production lines. The British weapons used in the trials are the Individual Weapon, now designated XL65E5, and the Light Support Weapon with the designation of XL65E4. Both fire the Radway Green 4.85mm XL2E1 ball round and the XL1E1 tracer round.

Netherlands The Dutch entry is the MN.1 assault rifle which is none other than the Israeli Galil rifle license-built in the Netherlands. It fires the standard M193 5.56mm cartridge.

West Germany Although it has now been withdrawn from the trials the West Germany entered their G11 individual weapon which fires the unconventional 4.75mm caseless round. (The earlier 4.3mm cartridges proved to produce too much barrel wear). The G11 was entered on a 'trials only' basis and development work is continuing on both the weapon and the cartridge which holds the projectile in a piece of high temperature propellant — once fired the propellant is entirely consumed. West Germany is also entering the MG3E as a light support weapon.

United States While the 5.56mm M16A1 rifle is being used as a control weapon for the trials it is also an entry firing the improved XM777 ball round. This new round has better trajectory performance and its penetration is improved by a steel insert. Considering the considerable political and economic 'muscle' that the United States can exert within NATO it seems very likely that this new cartridge will emerge as the new standard for nearly all Western Bloc nations. However the old 7.62mm round will still be retained for vehicle-mounted machine guns and for machine guns used in the heavy or long-range role. The United States will also enter their XM248 SAW machine gun for the support weapon trials.

As control weapons for the contest three existing weapons are being used. They are the American M16A1 (as mentioned above), the West German Heckler and Koch G3 firing the current 7.62mm cartridge, and the Belgian MAG light machine gun, also firing the 7.62mm cartridge. Ammunition trials have been carried out at Cold Meece in the United Kingdom, the weapon trials are being held at Meppen in West Germany and the same nation is the host for the weapon handling trials being held at Hammelburg. None of the trial results is held to be binding for any of the participants.

9mm PA3-DM Sub-Machine Gun   Argentina

Calibre: 9mm
Length: 70cm (with fixed butt)
69.3cm (with wire butt)
52.3cm (with wire butt retracted)
Length of barrel: 29cm
Weight: 3.9kg (loaded, with fixed butt)
3.95kg (loaded, with wire butt)
Mag capacity: 25 rounds
Muzzle velocity: 400m/s
Max effective range: 200m
Rate of fire: 650rpm (cyclic)

This weapon has been influenced in the design stage by the Israeli Uzi SMG and employs a similar pistol-grip magazine and a similar bolt extending over the barrel. It can be used with either a plastic butt or a sliding wire butt. Like most modern SMGs it can be used to fire grenades. It is in service with the Argentinian Army.

The 9mm PA3-DM SMG with butt extended.

9mm F1 Sub-Machine Gun   Australia

Calibre: 9mm
Length: 71.4cm
Length of barrel: 20.3cm
Weight: 4.47kg (loaded)
3.26kg (empty)
Mag capacity: 34 rounds
Muzzle velocity: 366m/s
Max effective range: 200m
Rate of fire: 600rpm (cyclic)
120rpm (practical)

The F1 was designed in 1959-1961 and went into production in 1962 to replace the Owen and Austen SMGs then in service. It is a conventional blow-back weapon with little of note apart from the vertically mounted curved magazine. When used in action in Vietnam its low-powered round was considered unsuitable and the type was replaced in front-line service with the American M-16A1.

The 9mm F1 SMG.

7.62mm L1A1-F1 Rifle

Australia

Calibre: 7.62mm
Length: 107.3cm
Length of barrel: 53.3cm
Weight: 4.91kg
Mag capacity: 20 rounds
Muzzle velocity: 838m/s
Max effective range: 600m
Rate of fire: 40rpm (single shots)

The Australian Small Arms Factory at Lithgow, New South Wales, produces the L1A1 rifle but also produces a special slightly shortened model for use with the small-statured defence forces of Papua and New Guinea. This is the L1A1-F1 and differs from the normal version by having a shortened butt and a revised muzzle flash eliminator.

Australian L1A1-F1 rifle.

7.62mm L2A1 Heavy-Barrelled Rifle

Australia

Calibre: 7.62mm
Length: 113.7cm
Length of barrel: 53.3cm
Weight: 6.9kg
Mag capacity: 30 rounds
Muzzle velocity: 838m/s
Range: 800m
Rate of fire: 650/700rpm (cyclic)
40rpm (single shots)

In addition to the L1A1 and L1A1-F1 rifles, the Lithgow plant has also produced a heavy-barrelled version of the L1A1 for use by Army units other than the Infantry (who still use the 7.62mm Bren along with the American M60). Designated the L2A1 the weapon has, apart from its heavy barrel, a bipod and an increased capacity magazine. Production of this model has now ceased.

Australian L2A1 heavy-barrelled rifle.

Calibre: .22in
Length: 90cm
64.5cm (without stock)
Length of barrel: 42.5cm
Weight: 4.5kg (loaded)
3.9kg (empty)
Mag capacity: 177 rounds
Range: 160m (max)
Rate of fire: 1,600rpm (cyclic)

Top the AM 180 with Laser Lok sight; centre the standard AM 180; below a new AM 180 with stock removed and a foregrip fitted.

The AM 180 has been developed by the American International Corporation of Salt Lake City, Utah, and is manufactured in Austria by the Voere Company. Over 1,000 have been sold, most of which have gone to police forces in the United States and elsewhere.

It fires from the open bolt using the blowback principle. The user can select either full automatic or semi-automatic and the weapon fires the standard .22in long rifle round with a m/v of 412m/s.

The forestock is of a durable plastic construction as is the removable stock. The fore sight is of the protected blade type and the rear sight is of the peep type and is adjustable in both the vertical and horizontal plane. According to the manufacturer, the main advantages of the AM 180 are that muzzle blast, barrel climb and barrel rotation are virtually non-existent. During trials, all 177 rounds were fired into a 7.5cm circle at a range of 18m.

A Laser Lok sight is also available for this weapon and this is mounted under the barrel. This provides pinpoint accuracy in dim light or night conditions by emitting a red dot that is about 7cm in diameter at 160m and indicates the point of impact.

The AM 180 is also available in a short barrel version with a folding shoulder stock.

The AM 180.

9mm Steyr-Daimler-Puch MPi 69 Sub-Machine Gun

Austria

Calibre: 9mm
Length: 67.3cm (butt extended)
47cm (butt retracted)
Length of barrel: 26cm
Weight: 3.52kg (loaded)
Mag capacity: 25 rounds
Muzzle velocity: 381m/s
Max effective range: 200m
Rate of fire: 400rpm (cyclic)

Despite the outward similarities with the Israeli Uzi SMG, the MPi 69 has many differences not the least of which is the unusual trigger mechanism. Instead of the usual two-position selector, the MPi 69 uses a dual-pressure trigger. A short squeeze will give single shots, while a definite pull-back will give full automatic fire. The cocking method is also unusual as it uses a backward pull on the sling which has to be held at right angles to the gun for the purpose. As well as the usual fixed sights, (two leaves at either 100 or 200m), a Singlepoint sight can be fitted as standard. This weapon is in service with the Austrian Army and has been evaluated by the Saudi-Arabian Forces.

The Steyr-Daimler-Puch 9mm MPi 69 SMG.

5.56mm Steyr-Daimler-Puch AUG Rifle

Austria

Calibre: 5.56mm
Length: 79cm
Length of barrel: 50cm
Weight: 3.3kg (empty)
Mag capacity: 30 rounds
Muzzle velocity: 950m/s
Max effective range: 400m
Rate of fire: 680rpm (cyclic)

The AUG (Armee-Universal-Gewehr) has been ordered for the Austrian forces with deliveries due to commence during 1978. Production is scheduled to continue until 1985 by which time 80,000 will have been produced. The construction of the AUG is unusual in that the entire weapon, apart from the barrel, bolt, chamber and mainspring, is made from toughened plastics (including the magazine) and light alloys. Carbine and LMG versions are projected.

7.62mm SSG 69 Sniper's Rifle

Austria

Calibre: 7.62mm
Length: 113cm
Length of barrel: 65cm
Weight: 4.5kg (with sight but without ammo)
Mag capacity: 5 rounds
Muzzle velocity: 860m/s
Range: 800m

The SSG 69 (Scharfschuetzengewehr 69) is the standard sniping rifle of the Austrian Army and is built by Steyr-Daimler-Puch. It fires a 7.62mm ×51mm cartridge and this weapon is also available commercially.

It is bolt-operated and fed from a five-round rotating spool magazine.

Its normal sights are a blade fore sight and a V-type back sight. Army models retain these but also have a Kahles Helia 6S2 telescopic sight with a magnification of ×6 which is graduated up to 800m.

If required, an infra-red or image-intensifier sight can be fitted in place of the telescopic sight.

7.62mm SSG 69 sniper's rifle.

9mm Browning HP Pistol

Belgium

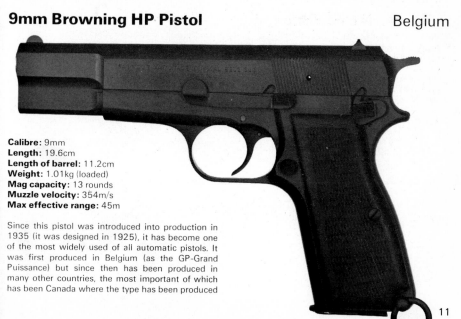

Calibre: 9mm
Length: 19.6cm
Length of barrel: 11.2cm
Weight: 1.01kg (loaded)
Mag capacity: 13 rounds
Muzzle velocity: 354m/s
Max effective range: 45m

Since this pistol was introduced into production in 1935 (it was designed in 1925), it has become one of the most widely used of all automatic pistols. It was first produced in Belgium (as the GP-Grand Puissance) but since then has been produced in many other countries, the most important of which has been Canada where the type has been produced

11

for military and civil use as the 'High Power'. The HP can be found with both fixed and ramp rear sights and some versions have provision for a butt stock. There are numerous variations and copies. The HP is in service with the British Army as the standard hand

weapon, and is used by many other armed forces. The type is still in widespread use in the Far East where many 'pirate' copies from a variety of sources remain in use. It is also built in Argentina (as the GP pistol) and the Indonesians built it as the Pindad.

9mm Mitraillette Vigneron M2 Sub-Machine Gun

Belgium

Calibre: 9mm
Length: 88.6cm (butt extended)
70.6cm (butt retracted)
Length of barrel: 30.5cm
Weight: 3.69kg (loaded)'
Mag capacity: 32 rounds
Muzzle velocity: 381m/s
Max effective range: 200m
Rate of fire: 620rpm (cyclic)

Designed by Colonel Vigneron, the M2 was adopted by the Belgian Army in 1953. Some remain in use in the Congo Republics and Luxembourg as well as with the Belgian Army.

The Mitraillette Vigneron 9mm M2 SMG.

5.56mm FN CAL Rifle

Belgium

Calibre: 5.56mm
Length: 98cm
115.3cm (with bayonet)
Length of barrel: 48.25cm
Weight: 3.3kg (total without mag)
3.85kg (with loaded 30-round steel mag)
3.7kg (with loaded 20-round steel mag)
Mag capacity: 20 or 30 rounds
Muzzle velocity: 895m/s
Max effective range: 400m
Rate of fire: 650-700rpm (cyclic)
120rpm (auto)
60rpm (single shots)

The 5.56mm FN CAL (Carbine Automatique Légère) was developed in the early 1960s and was one of the first European rifles to be built in 5.56mm calibre. Two models are available, one with a conventional stock and the other with a folding metal stock.

The weapon is gas-operated and the method of locking is the rotating-bolt method. The firer can select either full automatic, three-round bursts or single shots. Both 20- and 30-round magazines are

The FN 5.56mm CAL rifle.

available. The front sight is of the cylindrical post type and the rear sight is of the flip aperture type being graduated for 250 and 400m.

The CAL has three safety features:
1 Manual. The change lever axis acts directly on the trigger.

2 The safety sear frees the hammer only after the locking has taken place.
3 The firing pin, without spring, is held backward until the bolt is in the locking position.

The following accessories are available — removable bipod, bayonet and a blank firing device.

7.62mm FN FAL Rifle Belgium

Calibre: 7.62mm
Length: 200cm
Length of barrel: 53.3cm
Weight: 5.06kg (loaded)
4.31kg (empty)
Mag capacity: 20 rounds
Muzzle velocity: 823m/s
Max effective range: 600m
Rate of fire: 650-700rpm (cyclic)
120rpm (auto)
60rpm (single shots)

Design work on an automatic rifle in Belgium began before World War II and in 1949 a .280in 'Bull-pup' design was produced after experiments with a 7.92mm 'kurz' round model. With the demise of the .280in round the design was altered to a conventional layout and the result became known as the FN Fusil Automatique Légère, or FAL. In this form it became an enormous export success and a list of user countries is below. Manufacturing licences were taken up by several countries, one of the most important of which is the United Kingdom where the type was produced as the L1A1 with the automatic feature removed. There are many variations on the basic FAL theme as some models are fitted with

folding frame butts (LAR) and some versions are produced with heavy barrels and bipods to enable the weapon to be used as a LMG (eg: the Australian L2A1 and the Canadian Rifle, Automatic, FN C2A1). The FAL has a gas-operated mechanism, can be used to fire grenades, and a variety of accessories can be fitted.

User Nations — those marked with a * have manufacturing licences.

FN FAL Argentina*, Austria*, Barbados, Belgium*, Brazil, Burundi, Cambodia, Chile, Cuba, Dominica, Dubai, Ecuador, Gambia, Ghana, India*, Indonesia, Ireland, Israel*, Kuwait, Liberia, Libya, Luxembourg, Malawi, Morocco, Mozambique, Netherlands, Norway*, Paraguay, Peru, Portugal, South Africa*, West Germany.
L1A1 Australia*, Barbados, Canada*, Gambia, Guyana, Malaysia, Muscat, New Zealand, Singapore, United Kingdom*.

The 7.62mm L1A1 rifle being used by a British Soldier.

Above: The 7.62mm FN LAR with folding stock folded.

Below: The 7.62mm FN LAR with folding stock in the locked position.

Bottom: The 7.62mm FN FAL with bipod, heavy barrel and telescopic sights.

5.56mm FN Minimi Machine Gun   Belgium

Calibre: 5.56mm
Length: 100cm
Length of barrel: 46.8cm
Weight: 8.8kg (with 200 rounds)
6.5kg (with bipod but without mag)
6.2kg (without mag or ammo)
Mag capacity: 100 or 200 rounds
Muzzle velocity: 935m/s
Effective range: 500m
Rate of fire: 750/1,000rpm

The Minimi is the latest weapon to come from the FN stable. It has been designed to fire 5.56mm ammunition with a projectile weighing 3.6g, a 4g round has however been specially developed for the

Minimi and this will penetrate a steel helmet at a range of 800m. A tracer round with a m/v of 780m/s is under development. At a range of 400m the 4g round has a velocity of 507m/s and at 600m it is 310m/s.

The MG is gas-operated and the gas comes from the forward part of the barrel. The gas regulator has three positions — normal, emergency and grenade launching. The firer can select either full automatic fire or controlled bursts, ie 3-6 rounds. The barrel can be quickly replaced.

The weapon is available with a fixed stock, folding stock or without a stock for turret applications. A carrying handle is provided and the bipod can be folded up underneath the barrel if required. A tripod weighing 6kg is under development.

The ammunition is held together by disintegrating links and magazines holding 100 or 200 rounds are available; these are attached to the weapon.

The FN 5.56mm Minimi machine gun without magazine.

7.62mm FN MAG Machine Gun Belgium

Calibre: 7.62mm
Length: 125.5cm
Length of barrel: 54.5cm
Weight: 10.85kg (with bipod)
10.1kg (without butt and bipod)
Weight of tripod: 10.5kg
Type of feed: 50-round with belts
Continuous disintegrating link belts
Muzzle velocity: 840m/s
Max effective range: 1,200m
Rate of fire: 600-1,000rpm (cyclic)
250rpm (auto)

The FN MAG (Mitrailleuse à Gaz) was designed at Herstal during the early 1950s and soon became an export success to the extent that it is now in use all over the world. The United Kingdom took up a manufacturing licence and introduced some changes to produce the L7A1 series (qv). The FN MAG can be used either on a bipod or on a tripod for the extended fire role, for which role the quick barrel change feature is useful.

The 7.62mm FN MAG machine gun with tripod.

The 7.62mm FN MAG machine gun with bipod.

RL-100 Anti-Tank Weapon

Belgium

Calibre: 101mm
Weight: 12.9kg
Length: 188.5cm (deployed)
102cm (folded)
Range: 400m
Crew: 1

The RL-100 was designed and built by Mecar SA of Belgium. It is still used by the Belgian Army but is no longer in production.

A bipod is provided at the muzzle end of the weapon and it can be folded for easy transportation. It fires a HEAT round which weighs 2.75kg, has a muzzle velocity of 195m/s and will penetrate 400mm of armour.

The RL-100 anti-tank weapon.

RL-83 (Blindicide) Anti-Tank Weapon

Belgium

Calibre: 83mm
Weight: 8.4kg (with 900m sight)
Length: 170cm (in action)
92cm (folded)
Range: 900m (max)
400m (effective)
Crew: 1

The RL-83 was designed and built by Mecar SA of Belgium. It is still used by the Belgian Army but is no longer in production.

It can be fired from a bipod which is mounted at the forward part of the barrel or from the shoulder. A variety of rounds have been developed for the weapon including HEAT, illuminating, smoke, incendiary and anti-personnel.
The HEAT projectile has a m/v of 100m/s.
Three types of sight are available:
1 Standard metal sight for targets up to 400m.
2 Optical sight with same range as above.
3 Auxiliary sight to extend the range to 900m.

Weapons in Service with the People's Republic of China

The People's Republic of China armed forces employ a large range of infantry weapons many of which are locally made copies of weapons in service in the Soviet Bloc Armies. To prevent repetition a listing has been made of most of these types.

Pistols
7.62mm Type 51 (Copy of Tokarev TT33)
7.62mm Type 54 (Copy of Tokarev TT33)
9mm Type 59 (Copy of Makarov)

Sub-Machine Guns
7.62mm Type 50 (Copy of PPSh-41)
7.62mm Type 43 (Copy of PPS-43)

Rifles
7.62mm Type 53 Carbine (Copy of Model 1944 Carbine)
7.62mm Type 56 S.A. Carbine (Copy of SKS)
7.62mm Type 56 Assault Rifle (Copy of AK-47)
7.62mm Type 56-1 Assault Rifle (Copy of AK-47 with folding stock)

Light Machine Guns
7.62mm Type 53 (Copy of DPM)
7.62mm Type 56 (Copy of RPD)
7.62mm Type 58 (Copy of RP-46)

Medium Machine Gun
7.62mm Type 57 (Copy of SGM)

Heavy Machine Gun
12.7mm Type 54 (Copy of Model 38/46)

Light Mortars
60mm Type 31 (Copy of American 60mm M2 mortar)
60mm Type 63 (Revised Type 31)

Anti-Tank Weapons
87mm Type 51 (Copy of American 3.5in M20 rocket launcher)
57mm RR Type 36 (Copy of American M18 recoilless rifle)
40mm A/T Grenade Launcher Type 56 (Copy of Soviet RPG-2 weapon)
40mm A/T Grenade Launcher Type 69 (Copy of Soviet RPG-7 weapon)

The Chinese Type 56 assault rifle which is a copy of the Russian AK-47.

7.65mm Type 64 Silenced Pistol

China (PRC)

Calibre: 7.65mm
Length: 33cm
Length of barrel: 12.4cm
Weight: 1.27kg
Mag capacity: 8 rounds or single shot
Muzzle velocity: 274m/s
Max range: 35m

This unusual weapon has been developed purely as a close-range silent assassination weapon and it fires a unique 7.65mm × 17mm rimless round. Although it has an automatic mechanism, it would seem that it is intended primarily as a hand-operated single-shot weapon.

7.62mm Type 64 Silenced Sub-Machine Gun   China (PRC)

Calibre: 7.62mm
Length: 84.3cm (stock extended)
63.5cm (stock folded)
Length of barrel: 24.4cm
Weight: 3.4kg (empty)
Mag capacity: 30 rounds
Muzzle velocity: 513m/s
Max effective range: 135m
Rate of fire: 1,315rpm (cyclic)

mechanism has been copied from that of the Bren Gun while the bolt action is derived from the Russian PPS-43. The silencer is not completely effective but it has the virtue of hiding any flash while at the same time masking much of the muzzle blast noise. This weapon is in service with the Chinese armed forces and has seen action in Vietnam.

The Type 64 has a rather varied design origin as it seems to be made up of a number of design features from other weapons. For example, the trigger

7.62mm Type 64 silenced SMG with stock folded.

7.62mm Type 68 Rifle

China (PRC)

Calibre: 7.62 × 39mm
Length: 102.9cm
Length of barrel: 52.1cm
Weight: 3.49kg
Mag capacity: 15 rounds (normal) or
30 rounds (if modified)
Muzzle velocity: 730m/s
Max effective range: 400m (single shots)
200m (auto)
Rate of Fire: 750rpm (cyclic)
85rpm (auto)
40rpm (single shot)

Although the Type 68 outwardly resembles the Russian SKS it is a new Chinese design, and differs from the SKS in many ways not the least of which is the system of operation, which is not far removed from that used on the Russian AK-47. Early models of the Type 68 were machined from solid metal but the later, more widespread version, uses stamped steel assemblies. A typical Chinese/Eastern Bloc feature is the retention of a relatively long folding bayonet permanently attached to the underside of the barrel and forestock.

7.62mm Type 67 Light Machine Gun   China (PRC)

Calibre: 7.62mm
Length: 114.3cm
Length of barrel: 59.7cm
Weight: 8.8kg
Type of feed: 100-round link belt
Muzzle velocity: 835m/s
Max effective range: 800m
Rate of fire: 650rpm (cyclic)
150rpm (auto)

This weapon was designed to replace the large and varied number of types of machine gun in service in Communist China. It features a number of design features taken from existing designs and is gas-operated. It has been in action in Vietnam.

7.62mm Vzor 52 (Vz52) Pistol   Czechoslovakia

Calibre: 7.62mm
Length: 21cm
Length of barrel: 12cm
Weight: 1.045kg (with loaded 8-round mag)
.965kg (with empty 8-round mag)
.887kg (without mag)
Mag capacity: 8 rounds
Range: 50m

The Vz52 is an eight-shot, semi-automatic, short recoil-operated, magazine-fed weapon. It has been replaced to some extent by the Vz61 (Skorpion) machine pistol.

The Vz52 fires the 7.62mm × 25mm cartridge with a m/v of 492m/s. It is issued complete with a holster and a cleaning rod. Its fore sight is of the blade type and its rear sight is of the square notch type. The ejection port is on the RHS and the safety catch is on the LHS. The Vz50 is a 7.65mm pistol that is used by the Czechoslovakian Police and is similar to the German Walther PP/PPK weapons.

7.65mm M-61 Skorpion (Vzor 61) Machine Pistol   Czechoslovakia

Calibre: 7.65mm
Length: 51.3cm (with stock extended)
26.9cm (weapon only)
Length of barrel: 11.2cm
Weight: 1.55kg (with 20-round mag)
1.45kg (with 10-round mag)
1.29kg (without mag)
Mag capacity: 10- or 20-round mag
Range: 100/200m (with stock, semi-auto)
50m (with stock, auto)
Rate of Fire: 750rpm (cyclic)

The Vzor 61 is a blowback operated weapon that is capable of both full automatic or semi-automatic fire. The weapon can be used as a pistol or with its stock as a light SMG. The metal stock folds through 180° when not required. The Vzor fires the standard 7.65mm Browning commercial cartridge with a m/v of 317m/s. When being used on automatic its practical rate of fire is 100rpm and when on semi-automatic its practical rate of fire is 35rpm. The selector is on the LHS and has the marking 20 for automatic fire and 1 for single shots as well as for safe. If required, it can be fitted with a bayonet, silencer and luminous sights for use at night. The fore sight is of the cylindrical post type and the rear sight is of the flip type with two settings, one for 75m and the other for 150m. Both hip and shoulder holsters are available for the Vzor 61.

The 7.65mm M-61 Skorpion machine pistol.

9mm M23 and M25 (Vzor 23 and Vzor 25) Czechoslovakia
Sub-Machine Guns

Data: Vzor 25
Calibre: 9mm
Length: 68.6cm (stock extended)
44.5cm (stock folded)
Length of barrel: 28.4cm
Weight: 4.1kg (with loaded 40-round mag)
4.06kg (with loaded 24-round mag)
3.68kg (with empty 40-round mag)
3.64kg (with empty 24-round mag)
3.4kg (without mag)

Mag capacity: 24 or 40 rounds
Range: 150m (semi-auto)
100m (auto)
Rate of fire: 650rpm (cyclic)
50rpm (semi-auto)
80/100rpm (auto)

The 9mm M23 SMG with fixed wooden stock.

These weapons entered service with the Czechoslovakian Army after World War II, and remained until they were replaced by the similar M24 and M26 weapons. These are chambered for 7.62mm cartridges. The M23 has a fixed wooden stock and the M25 a folding metal stock. They both fire the 9mm × 19mm Parabellum cartridge with a m/v of 450m/s and their box magazines go straight up through the handle. They can be fired either semi-automatic or full automatic; the type of fire is

The 9mm M25 SMG with folding metal stock.

controlled by the amount of pressure that is applied to the trigger. An unusual feature is that the bolt is hollow and overrides the barrel, this permits the use of a longer barrel for better ballistic performance without lengthening the weapon itself.

7.62mm M24 and M26 (Vzor 24 and Vzor 26) Sub-Machine Guns   Czechoslovakia

Calibre: 7.62mm
Length: 68.5cm
Length of barrel: 28.5cm
Weight: 3.98kg (with loaded 32-round mag)
3.64kg (with empty 32-round mag)
3.38kg (with no mag)
Mag capacity: 32 rounds
Range: 150m (semi-auto)
100 (auto)
Rate of Fire: 650rpm (cyclic)
80/100rpm (auto)
50rpm (semi-auto)

This is basically the M23 and M25 9mm sub-machine guns chambered to fire the 7.62mm × 25P round with a m/v of 550m/s. Apart from the change in calibre they have a heavier bolt and a new magazine to take the longer 7.62mm round. They are distinguishable from the earlier weapons as their magazines have a forward pitch. The M24 has a wooden stock and the M26 a folding metal stock. Like the earlier weapons, they are of rugged, simple construction, much use being made of stamped parts.

7.62mm URZ Small-Arms System   Czechoslovakia

	AP	LK	TK	T
Calibre:	7.62mm	7.62mm	7.62mm	7.62mm
Length:	99.5cm	99.5cm	120cm	87.7cm
Weight:	3.9kg	5.2kg	11kg (with tripod)	5.6kg
Mag capacity:	50 rounds	50 rounds	250-round belt	belt
Muzzle velocity:	717m/s	717m/s	800m/s	800m/s
Rate of fire (cyclic):	800rpm	800rpm	800rpm	1,100rpm
Rate of fire (auto):	150rpm	120rpm	200rpm	200rpm

The URZ (Universal Small-Arms) system was introduced by Ceskoslovenska Zbrojovka in 1970 but has not so far been placed in quantity production. All weapons in the family are gas operated and fire a 7.62mm × 39mm cartridge although they could also be chambered for the NATO 7.62mm × 51mm cartridge. The range comprises an automatic rifle (AP) light machine gun (LK), medium machine gun (TK) and a tank machine gun (T) All of the weapons (except the tank model) have adjustable fore sights and leaf back sights, are fed from a 50-round magazine (or in the case of the TK, belt fed as well), and have a grenade sight permanently fitted to the fore sight stock. The LK has a quick change barrel, carrying handle and a folding bipod. The medium machine gun is a tripod version of the LK and is fed from a 250-round belt and is provided with an optical sight, if required the bipod can be quickly converted in an anti-aircraft mount. The tank machine gun is solenoid controlled and belt fed. The optical sight of the medium machine gun can also be mounted on the rifle and the light machine gun.

7.62mm Vzor 58 (Vz58P or Vz58V) Assault Rifle Czechoslovakia

Data: Vz58P
Calibre: 7.62mm
Length: 100cm (with bayonet)
84.5cm (rifle only)
65cm (Vz58V with stock folded)
Length of barrel: 39cm
Weight: 3.77kg (loaded with bayonet)
3.59kg (loaded without bayonet)
3.28kg (with empty mag and bayonet)
3.1kg (with empty mag)
2.91kg (without mag)
.68kg (loaded mag)
.19kg (empty mag)
.18kg (bayonet)
Mag capacity: 30 rounds
Range: 300m
Rate of fire: 800/820rpm (cyclic)
80/100rpm (auto)
40rpm (semi-auto)

The Vzor 58 is the standard assault rifle of the Czechoslovakian Army having been introduced into service in 1958. It is a gas-operated, magazine-fed weapon and although it is similar in appearance to the Soviet AK-47 the design is different. The Vz58 has a swinging-wedge breech-lock and a plunger type hammer whereas the AK-47 has a rotary bolt and a swinging hammer. The Vz58 fires the same 7.62mm × 39mm cartridge as the AK-47 although their magazines are not interchangeable.

The Vz58P has the conventional fixed stock and is also known as the M58P. The Vz58V has a folding metal buttstock and is also known as the M58V. There are a number of accessories for this weapon including a sling, bayonet, flash-hider, bipod, sectional cleaning rod, magazine carrier, front sight wrench and it can also be fitted with the NSP-2 infra-red sight for night operations.

The 7.62mm Vz58P assault rifle with conventional stock.

7.62mm M52 and M52/57 Semi-Automatic Rifle

Czechoslovakia

Data: M52/57
Calibre: 7.62mm
Length: 120.5cm (with bayonet)
100.5cm (rifle only)
Length of barrel: 52.3cm
Weight: 4.53kg (with loaded mag)
4.25kg (with empty mag)
4.1kg (without mag)
Mag capacity: 10 rounds
Range: 400m

The M52 and M52/57 semi-automatic rifles were once the standard equipment of the Czechoslovakian Army. They have now been replaced in front-line service by the M58 assault rifle.

The M52 and the M52/57 are mechanically identical, both have a permanently attached folding knife bayonet on the RHS. The gas operation of the rifle is somewhat similar to the German World War II Gew 41 rifle in that the gas cylinder completely encircles the barrel. The trigger assembly is identical in operation to that of the American M1 rifle.

The M52 fires the Czechoslovakian 7.62mm × 45mm cartridge which is also used for the Czech M52 LMG, this has a m/v of 744m/s, practical rate of fire is 25rpm. It is sighted to 1,000m with intervals of 50m. The M52/57 is chambered for the Soviet 7.62mm × 39mm cartridge with a m/v of 735m/s. It is sighted to only 900m.

The 7.62mm M52/57 semi-automatic rifle.

7.62mm M54 Sniper's Rifle

Czechoslovakia

Calibre: 7.62mm
Length: 114.8cm
Length of barrel: 73.2cm
Weight: 4.1kg (with loaded mag and 'scope)
4kg (with empty mag and 'scope)
Mag capacity: 10 rounds
Range: 1,000m (max with 'scope)
800m (max combat range)
Rate of fire: 10rpm

The M54 is similar in appearance to the Soviet M1891/30 rifle but has been cut down to resemble a sporting rifle. It is fitted with a telescopic sight and fires the 7.62mm × 54R cartridge with a m/v of 811m/s. It may well have been replaced by the more recent Soviet SVD 7.62mm sniper's rifle.

7.62mm Vzor 59 (Vz59L, Vz59 and Vz59N) General Purpose Machine Gun

Czechoslovakia

	M-59	M-59L
Calibre:	7.62mm	7.62mm
Length:	128cm	118.5cm
Length of barrel:	69.3cm	59.3cm
Weight:	19.5kg	——— (with tripod)
	9.37kg	8.77kg (with bipod)
	1.946kg	1.946kg (ammo box with 50 rounds)
	9.15kg	9.15kg (ammo box with 250 rounds)
Range:	1,300m	900m (effective)
	4,800m	4,800m (max)
Rate of fire:	700/850	700/850rpm (cyclic)
	300	150rpm (practical)

The Vz59 is the standard machine gun of the Czechoslovakian Army but is not used by any other Warsaw Pact Forces. It fires the 7.62mm ×54R cartridge with a m/v of 760/790m/s. It is also available for export (Vz59N) and the export model fires the 7.62mm × 51mm NATO cartridge.

The Vz59L has a short barrel and is provided with a bipod, the 50-round box magazine is attached to the weapon and a carrying handle is provided. The basic Vz59 has the longer and heavier barrel and is normally mounted on a tripod which can also be adopted for the anti-aircraft role very quickly. When used on the tripod it is fed from a 250-round box which is to the right of the weapon. If required the Vz59 can be fitted with the lighter barrel and mounted on a bipod. It has a pillar type front sight and V-notch rear sight adjustable from 100m to 2,000m in 100m increments.

The Vz59 and Vz59L can be fitted with a ×4 telescopic sight or the PPN-2 infra-red night sight.

The Vz59T is a AFV machine gun and this is fitted to the OT-62 and OT-810 APCs.

The Vz59N GPMG.

7.62mm Vzor 52 (Vz52) and Vzor 52/57 (Vz52/57) Light Machine Gun

Czechoslovakia

Data: Vz52/57
Calibre: 7.62mm
Length: 104.5cm
Length of barrel: 58.3cm
Weight: 8.7kg (with loaded mag)
8.3kg (with empty mag)
8kg (without mag)
Mag capacity: 25-round box or a 100-round belt
Range: 800m
Rate of fire: 900rpm (cyclic) box magazine
1,140rpm (cyclic) belt fed
150rpm (practical)

The Vz52 LMG.

The Vz52 was introduced into service in 1952 and was a development of the earlier Vz26 weapon (similar to the British Bren). The Vz52 is a selective fire, gas-operated air-cooled weapon. Its barrel can be quickly changed, if required the gun can be mounted on a tripod in place of its normal bipod. The Vz52 fires the Czech 7.62mm × 45mm M52 cartridge with a m/v of 755m/s. It has no selector as such, the rate of fire being determined by the position of the gunner's finger on the trigger, the upper part of the trigger (marked 1) for single shots and the lower part of the trigger (marked D) for full automatic. Yet another feature of the Vz52 is that it is cocked by pulling the pistol grip to the rear. The fore sight is of the blade type and the rear sight is of the tangent type with a U-notch, this is graduated from 200 to 1,200m in increments of 100m.

The Vz52 is no longer in front-line service with the Czech Army.

In 1957 the Vz52/57 was introduced into service; this fires the 7.62mm × 39R cartridge with a m/v of 732m/s. Accessories for these weapons include a fabric sling, magazine carrier, belt boxes, combination tool and cleaning rod. The Vz52/59 was replaced in front-line units from 1959/60 with the 7.62mm Vz59 GPMG.

7.92mm ZB-26 and ZB-30 Light Machine Guns

Czechoslovakia

Data: ZB-26
Calibre: 7.92mm
Length: 116.3cm
Length of barrel: 61cm
Weight: 9.6kg (with loaded mag)
9.1kg (with empty mag)
8.9kg (without mag)
Mag capacity: 20 rounds
Range: 800m
Rate of fire: 500rpm (cyclic)
180rpm (practical)

The ZB-26 was issued to the Czechoslovakian Army before the start of World War II and was also used as the basis for the Bren LMG. The Czechs continued to use this weapon after the war until it was replaced by the Vz52 LMG. The weapon fires the 7.92mm × 57mm cartridge with a m/v of 810m/s. The gun is gas operated and air-cooled and can fire both on full automatic or single shots. Its front sight is of the blade type and its rear sight is of the adjustable aperture type. Both the ZB-26 and the ZB-30 were used by the Germans during World War II as they continued production of the gun. The ZB-26 was also built for export as the ZB-30 whose most obvious modification was that it could be fitted with a monopod in a socket in the stock. The ZB-30 was also built in China as the Type 26 LMG; in addition Iran and Romania built the weapon. Yugoslavia also built the ZB-30. The ZB-26 is recognisable by its flash eliminator, ribbed barrel, gas cylinder under the barrel, bipod, carrying handle above the barrel and in front of the vertical magazine and the barrel locking handle on the LHS of the weapon.

The Czech ZB-26 LMG.

7.92mm ZB-37 Machine Gun

Czechoslovakia

Calibre: 7.92mm
Length: 110.5cm
Length of barrel: 74cm (with flash eliminator)
67.8cm (barrel only)
Weight: 39kg (gun and tripod)
19kg (gun only)
Mag capacity: Fed from 100- or 200-round
metallic non-disintegrating link belt
Range: 1,000m (max effective)
Rate of fire: 750rpm (high setting)
500rpm (low setting)
200rpm (practical)

The ZB-37 was introduced into service with the
Czech Army in 1937 and was used by them after the
war. It is no longer in service with any of the Warsaw

Pact Forces but it did turn up in the fighting in
Nigeria a few years ago. The Germans used the
weapon during World War II and called it the
MG 37(t), the British adopted the weapon for use as
a tank machine gun under the name Besa and this is
no longer in service with the British Army. The ZB-37
fires the 7.92mm × 57mm cartridge with a m/v of
793m/s. Its fore sight is of the blade type and its rear
sight is of the leaf type graduated from 300 to
2,000m. The weapon can be found with both a
smooth or a ribbed barrel and there are two types of
tripod.

82mm T-21 (Tarasnice) Recoilless Gun

Czechoslovakia

Calibre: 82mm
Weight of launcher: 20kg (travelling, with wheel
mount)
17.2kg (firing, without wheel mount)
Length of tube: 147.5cm
Range: 280m (moving target)
Rate of fire: 4-6rpm
Crew: 2

The T-21 is an electrically-fired, smooth-bore
breech-loaded recoilless weapon that can be fired
from the ground using the two small detachable
wheels for support or from the shoulder whilst
standing or in the prone position. The weapon has
also been mounted externally on the turrets of the
OT-62 armoured personnel carrier and the OT-65
reconnaissance vehicle.

It is recognisable by its two small wheels, the
towing handle that folds back along the tube at the
front and the two pistol type grips.

The weapon fires a fin-stabilised HEAT projectile
which has a Z-21 fuse. The projectile weighs 2.13kg,
has a muzzle velocity of 250m/s and will penetrate
230mm of armour. The T-21 is provided with two
sights on the LHS, one is optical and the other is
mechanical. The optical sight is marked from 100 to
600m in 100m intervals whilst the mechanical
sights is marked from 100 to 600m in 50m intervals.

Since the breechblock has no extractor, the loader
must either shake out the expended case or extract it
with the aid of an asbestos glove.

The 82mm T-21 Tarasnice recoilless gun.

P-27 (Pancerovka) Anti-Tank Grenade Launcher

Czechoslovakia

Calibre: 45mm (tube)
Weight of launcher: 6.4kg
Length of tube: 103cm
Range: 100m (stationary target)
75mm (moving target)
Rate of fire: 4-6rpm
Crew: 2

The P-27 is the Czech equivalent of the Russian RPG-2 weapon. The ammunition cannot be used in the Soviet weapon, however. It is a smooth-bore, muzzle-loaded, recoilless weapon and its recognition features are its bipod which unfolds, pistol type grip and folding sights.

The HEAT round is not rocket-assisted and is 720mm in length and weighs 3.75kg; the projectile weighs 3.3kg and has a muzzle velocity of 75m/s and will penetrate 250mm of armour.

The sights are marked for 50, 75, 100, 125 and 150m, and the firing mechanism is by electricity generated by a magneto. The P-27 has been replaced in front-line Czech units by the Soviet RPG-7V weapon.

The P-27 (Pancerovka) anti-tank grenade launcher.

9mm Madsen Model 50 and 53 Sub-Machine Guns

Denmark

Data: Model 50
Calibre: 9mm
Length: 79.37cm (stock extended)
52.83cm (stock folded)
Length of barrel: 19.8cm
Weight: 3.2kg (empty)
Mag capacity: 32 rounds
Muzzle velocity: 390m/s
Max effective range: 100m
Rate of fire: 550rpm (cyclic)

The Madsen Model 50 and 53 are basically similar and have a number of unusual design features. One is the method of stripping which is effected by removing the magazine and barrel nut when the two receiver halves then open sideways on two hinges at the rear. The magazine can be filled using a filler-guide carried in the pistol grip. Both types were developed from the earlier Model 1946 and both have been sold to various forces around the world including Chile.

A version of the Madsen is made in Brazil as the Metralhadora de MAO .45in INA 953. This version, apart from the .45in calibre, differs in many respects from the original but is visually similar. It is used by the Brazilian Army and police.

9mm Lahti M35 Pistol Finland

Calibre: 9mm
Length: 24.6cm
Length of barrel: 10.7cm
Weight: 1.22kg
Mag capacity: 8 rounds
Muzzle velocity: 350m/s
Max effective range: 40m

Despite the fact that it was first accepted for service in 1935, the Lahti is still in service in Finland, and is also still in use in Sweden where it is known as the P40 or M40. The mechanism of the Lahti is very reliable and well-sealed to keep out dirt and grit but it is a very difficult weapon to strip — two factors which may explain its longevity.

Top the Finnish Lahti L/35 pistol compared to the lower Swedish Husqvarna P-40 or M40 pistol.

9mm Model 1944 Sub-Machine Gun   Finland

Calibre: 9mm
Length: 83.1cm (stock extended)
62.2cm (stock folded)
Weight: 3.59kg (with loaded 36-round mag)
4.27kg (with loaded 71-round drum)
2.9kg (empty)
Mag capacity: 36-round box
71-round drum
Muzzle velocity: 399m/s
Max effective range: 200m
Rate of fire: 650rpm (cyclic)

The Model 1944 was a Finnish copy of the Russian PPS-43 to take the 9mm Parabellum round and it was built in Finland in large quantities before the war

ended. In appearance if differs little from the Russian original, but in Finnish Army service it is usually used with the 36-round box magazine — the 50-round Suomi and 71-round Russian magazines may also be used. The designer later took the drawings to Spain where the type was made at Oviedo as the Dux SMG. This weapon was licence-built by Mauser and later Anshutz for the West German Border Guard where it is still in use in small numbers.

9mm Model 1931 (m/31) Sub-Machine Gun   Finland

Calibre: 9mm
Length: 87cm
Length of barrel: 31.8cm
Weight: 7.09kg (with 71-round mag)
4.68kg (without mag)
Mag capacity: 50-round box
71-round drum
Muzzle velocity: 399m/s
Effective range: 200m
Rate of fire: 900rpm (cyclic)
120rpm (auto)
40rpm (single shots)

The Model 1931 SMG was made in Finland by Oy Tikkakoski and was subsequently adopted by a number of countries including Norway, Sweden and Switzerland (known as the MP 43/44).

Its system of operation is of the blowback type and it fires a standard 9mm Parabellum cartridge. The firer can select either full automatic fire or single shots.

A Finnish soldier using his m/31 SMG with a 71-round drum type magazine.

7.62mm M60 and M62 Assault Rifles   Finland

Calibre: 7.62mm
Length: 91.4cm
Length of barrel: 42cm
Weight: 4.7kg (loaded)
3.5kg (empty)
Mag capacity: 30 rounds
Muzzle velocity: 719m/s
Max effective range: 350-400m
Rate of fire: 650rpm (cyclic)
120rpm (auto)
40rpm (single shots)

During the late 1950s the Finnish Valmet concern acquired a manufacturing licence to make the Russian AK-47 assault rifle. Before the weapon could be accepted by the Finnish Army some changes were called for and the result was the M60. This differs from the AK-47 in having no trigger-guard (to accommodate winter mittens), no wooden furniture (all the stocks and grips are plastic) and revised sights. Another change is the tubular butt. The M62 differs in small detail, the most noticeable of which is the reintroduction of the trigger-guard.

The Finnish 7.62mm M62 assault rifle.

7.62mm and 5.56mm M76 Assault Rifles   Finland

	M76	M76T	M76M
Calibre:	7.62mm	7.62mm	7.62mm
Length:	94.5cm	94.4cm	94.5cm
Length (butt folded):	N/A	46.7cm	N/A
Weight (without mag):	3.6kg	3.75kg	3.6kg
Weight (with loaded mag):	4.5kg	4.66kg	4.51kg

Further development of the M62 by Valmet has resulted in the new M76 series of assault rifles which are available in both 7.62mm (7.62mm × 39mm) and 5.56mm (5.56mm × 45mm) calibres. Four basic models are available, the M76 with a tubular fixed buttstock, M76M with a plastic buttstock, M76T with a folding metal butt stock and a version with a fixed wooden stock. All are gas operated and have a cyclic rate of fire of 650rpm, practical rate of fire is 20-40rpm and the firer can select single shots or full automatic. In addition to the normal day sights the rifle is fitted with specially built-in night sights.

Valmet offer the following accessories for these weapons: 15- or 30-round magazines, knife, bayonet, with scabbard, sling and magazine-carrying pouch for two loaded magazines.

The company is now designing a heavy version of the M76 which can be used as a light machine gun; this will have a heavier and longer barrel, bipod and will be fed from a 75-round drum magazine, it will also accept the standard 30-round magazine.

Valmet 7.62mm M76T with metal stock folded and showing both 15- and 30-round magazines.

Valmet M76T stripped to show main components.

7.62mm KK62 Light Machine Gun

Finland

Calibre: 7.62mm
Length: 108.5cm
Length of barrel: 47cm
Weight: 10.6kg (loaded)
8.5kg (empty)
Type of feed: 100-round belt
Muzzle velocity: 730m/s
Max effective range: 350-450m
Rate of fire: 1,000-1,100rpm (cyclic)
300rpm (practical)

Despite the lack of external similarities, the KK62 is based on the mechanism of the Czech ZB26 LMG. It entered service with the Finnish Army in 1966 and

has also been adopted by Qatar. For an LMG the KK62 has a high rate of fire and is also unusual in feeding the 7.62mm × 39mm Russian cartridge belts from the RHS. Only full automatic fire is possible — there is no facility for single shots. No trigger-guard is fitted in line with Finnish practice to allow for the use of thick gloves by the firer. Accessories include a belt pouch, cleaning and tool kit and a sling.

The Valmet 7.62mm KK62 light machine gun which is used by Finland and Qatar.

Type m/55 Anti-Tank Grenade Launcher

Finland

Calibre: 55mm
Length: 94cm (without grenade)
124cm (with grenade)
Weight: 6.5kg (launcher only)
2.5kg (grenade)
Effective range: 300m
Rate of fire: 3-5rpm

The m/55 is the standard light anti-tank weapon of the Finnish Army and is similar in some respects to the Soviet RPG-7 launcher. The sight is on the LHS with the handle and firing trigger in the centre; at the rear is the venturi. The HEAT grenade is reported to be able to penetrate 300mm of armour at 300m.

9mm PAP Mle F1 Pistol France

Calibre: 9mm
Length: 23.4cm
Length of barrel: 15cm
Weight: 1.215kg (empty)
Mag capacity: 15 rounds
Muzzle velocity: 350m/s
Max effective range: 50m

The 9mm PAP Mle F1 is the service version of the 9mm MAB P15s. It is a remarkable service pistol in that it has a 15-round magazine which together with the long barrel employed make it a very good target pistol. As well as being in service with the French Army it is also used by the French Air Force.

9mm MAS Model 1950 Pistol France

Calibre: 9mm
Length: 19.5cm
Length of barrel: 11.1cm
Weight: 1.04kg (loaded)
.81kg (empty)
Mag capacity: 9 rounds
Muzzle velocity: 354m/s
Max effective range: 50m

As well as being in service with the French Army, the Model 1950 is also in use with the French Gendarmerie and Police.

9mm MAT 49 Sub-Machine Gun

France

Calibre: 9mm
Length: 71cm (butt extended)
55.8cm (butt retracted)
Weight: 4.76kg (loaded)
Mag capacity: 32 rounds
Muzzle velocity: 354m/s
Max effective range: 200m
Rate of fire: 600rpm (cyclic)

The MAT 49 is made from heavy gauge steel pressings and features an unusual magazine which can be folded forward to reduce bulk when carried. A grip safety is employed so there is no safety catch. The MAT 49 is now the standard SMG of the French forces, and is still in use by some of the former French Colonies in Africa. The Vietnamese have converted some MAT 49s to fire the Soviet 7.62mm × 25m cartridge.

5.56mm MAS Automatic Rifle

France

Calibre: 5.56mm
Length: 75.7cm
Length of barrel: 48.8cm
Weight: 3.38kg (less mag and extras)
Mag capacity: 25 rounds
Muzzle velocity: 960m/s
Max effective range: 300m
Rate of fire: 900-1,000rpm (cyclic)

The MAS rifle is a new design using a 'bullpup' configuration with optional ejection to left or right. The large handle over the barrel also acts as a protective cover for the sights. This handle and the butt are both plastic. The trigger mechanism can be set to either single shots or automatic but an extra mode can be selected that fires a three-round burst every time the trigger is pressed. Bipod legs can be fitted and grenades can also be fired. The MAS has been adopted by the French Army.

The 5.56mm MAS automatic rifle with Bipod.

FR-F1 Sniper's Rifle

France

Calibre: 7.5mm and 7.62mm
Length: 113.8cm (variable)
Weight: 5.2kg (empty)
Mag capacity: 10 rounds
Muzzle velocity: 852m/s
Max effective range: 800m

The FR-F1, or Fusil a Repetition Modele F1, is a version of the prewar Model 1936 rifle modified to take telescopic sights for use by snipers. It has a manual bolt action and butt spacers can be fitted to the butt to suit individual requirements. To suit the sniper role, two extras are a bipod and a flash hider. Some of these rifles were produced in 7.62mm calibre.

The French 7.5mm FR-F1 sniper's rifle with bipod and telescopic sight.

7.5mm Model 49/56 Rifle

France

Calibre: 7.5mm
Length: 101cm
Length of barrel: 52.1cm
Weight: 4.34kg (loaded)
Mag capacity: 10 rounds
Muzzle velocity: 817m/s
Max effective range: 600m

The MAS 49/56 self-loading rifle was developed from the earlier Model 49 from which it differs in having a shortened forestock and a combined flash hider and grenade launcher. It is at present the standard French service rifle and it is also used in many former French Dependencies. The earlier Model 49 also remains in widespread use. A telescopic sight can be fitted. Some Model 49/56 rifles were produced in NATO 7.62mm calibre.

The 7.5mm Model 49/56 rifle.

7.5mm AA 52 Machine Gun

France

Calibre: 7.5mm and 7.62mm
Length: 114.5cm (with light barrel)
50cm (length of light barrel)
60cm (length of heavy barrel)
Weight: 10.7kg (with light barrel and bipod)
Type of feed: Continuous link belts
Muzzle velocity: 800m/s
Max range: 3,000m
Rate of fire: 800rpm (cyclic)

The 'Arme Automatique Transformable Mle 1952' is the standard French machine gun and is unusual in many respects. It uses a form of retarded blow-back action and is one of the very few machine guns to employ this type of action with a full-power cartridge. As a result the chamber walls are fluted for ease of extraction but examination of fired cartridges will often show distortion or even breakage. The general standard of manufacture shows that the weapon has been designed for low cost and many stampings are used. In the LMG role a light barrel and bipod are used — this is the Fusil-Mitrailleur N-F1. As a sustained fire weapon the gun is fitted with a heavy barrel and mounted on a tripod. In both roles the gun can fire automatic only. As an LMG the gun can be laid on fixed lines by the use of a telescopic monopod leg under the butt. The AA 52 has been produced in both 7.5mm and 7.62mm calibres.

The 7.5mm AA 52 machine gun.

68mm SARPAC Anti-Tank Rocket Launcher

France

Calibre: 68mm
Length: 73.4cm (carrying)
99.7cm (ready for action)
Weight: 2.67kg (carrying, with rocket)
2.35kg (ready for action, with rocket)
Range: 150-200m
Crew: 1 or 2

The SARPAC is a light infantry support weapon which is manufactured by Hotchkiss-Brandt. When required for action the covers at either end of the barrel are removed, the barrel is extended and the sights raised. When firing anti-personnel and illuminating rockets an additional telescope is used, as these are fired at an angle of up to 40°.

The following fin-stabilised rockets are available for the SARPAC launcher: Rochar anti-tank rocket weighing 1.07kg. This is 47.2cm in length and has a range of 200m; muzzle velocity is 150m/s and its shaped charged warhead will penetrate 300mm of armour. Like the anti-personnel rocket, the anti-tank rocket is not armed until it is 10/12m out of the launcher.

Rocap anti-personnel rocket weighing 1.8kg has a maximum range of 630m and has good fragmentation.

Roclair illuminating rocket weighing 1.3kg, will illuminate a 300m diameter zone for 30 seconds with an average power of 180,000 candelas.

The SARPAC 68mm anti-tank launcher: top shows the launcher ready for action, No 1 is the Rochar anti-tank rocket, No 2 is the Rocap anti-personnel rocket and No 3 is the Roclair illuminating rocket, the bottom photograph shows the SARPAC ready for carrying.

89mm STRIM Anti-Tank Rocket Launcher France

Calibre: 88.9mm
Length: 116.8cm (carrying)
160cm (ready for action)
Weight: 4.5kg (carrying including telescope)
7.3kg (ready for action)
Range: 200-600m (practical)
2,300m (max at 45° angle)
Crew: 2

This weapon has been developed by Luchaire SA and is manufactured in cooperation with the Manufacture Nationale d'Armes de Saint-Etienne, and is marketed by Hotchkiss-Brandt.

The rocket launcher itself is of glass fibre construction and is reusable.

When required for action a rocket in its container is attached to the rear of the launcher, as this is done the firing circuit is connected. The rocket is kept in a sealed container which is 62.6cm in length and weighs a total of 3.2kg. The rocket itself weighs 2.2kg and has a shaped charge warhead 80mm in diameter. The rocket has a muzzle velocity of 300m/s and will, according to the manufacturers, penetrate 400mm of armour or concrete.

As the rocket leaves the launcher nine stabilisers unfold and these stabilise the rocket in flight. Flight time to 330m = 1.25sec and flight time to 360m = 1.36 sec.

The STRIM is fitted with the APX M 290 sighting system which is graduated from 0 to 1,000m, a passive telescope for night action is also available. Other rockets available apart from the basic anti-tank model, are a practice rocket, an illuminating rocket, an incendiary rocket and the AVL light anti-tank rocket.

60mm Hotchkiss-Brandt (MO-60-63) Light Mortar
France

Calibre: 60mm
Length of barrel: 72.4cm (including breech)
Weight: 14.8kg (total)
3.8kg (barrel)
5kg (bipod)
6kg (baseplate)
Elevation: +40° to +85°
Traverse: 30mils
Range: 100m (min)
2,050m (max)
Crew: 3

The MO-60-63 is manufactured by the Armament Department of Hotchkiss-Brandt. It has been designed so that it can be broken down into three-man pack loads for easy transportation: barrel, bipod and baseplate. This mortar can fire the old 60mm Brandt bombs and the 60mm American bombs. Hotchkiss-Brandt manufacture the following bombs for it.
HE Bomb Mk 61: This has a V 9 fuse and weighs 1.78kg
HE Coloured Bomb: Green, yellow or red.
Smoke Bomb Mk 61.
Practice Bomb: Two types.
Illuminating Bomb Mk 61: Weight 1.55kg.
180,000 candelas.

The bombs have a primary and secondary charge system which gives six charges, ie charge 0 = 100m range and charge 5 = 2,050m range normal rate of fire is 20rpm although 30rpm can be fired for short

The Hotchkiss-Brandt 60mm light mortar in the assembled position.

periods. These bombs are also used with the Hotchkiss-Brandt 60mm Commando Mortar, but with this weapon No 2 charge is the maximum that can be used.

60mm Hotchkiss-Brandt Commando Mortar
France

Calibre: 60mm
Length: 68cm (overall, auto model)
86.1cm (overall, controlled firing model)
Length of barrel: 65cm
Weight: 7.7kg (auto model)
10kg (controlled firing model)

Range: 100m (min)
1,050m (max)
Crew: 2

This light hand-held weapon is manufactured by the Armament Department of Hotchkiss-Brandt. It consists of the following parts — barrel, breech, baseplate, protective sleeve, muzzle cover and carrying strap. The weapon is normally carried fully assembled with the aid of the strap. It fires the same bombs as the Hotchkiss-Brandt 60mm Light Mortar (MO-60-63) (qv). For use with the Commando mortar three charges are used 0, 1 and 2, ie charge 0 - 100m range and charge 2 = 1,050m range. Charge 3 can be used in 'exceptional circumstances.'

The weapon is normally loaded, aimed and fired from the lying or kneeling position. Two models are available, the automatic model and the controlled firing model. The difference between the two models is that the standard model (automatic) is fired as a normal mortar, ie the bomb is dropped down the barrel where it hits a firing pin and is then fired. In the controlled model the bomb is dropped down the barrel and is fired when required by pressing the trigger.

The standard model has a simple clinometer and range table which the controlled model does not have.

The controlled model is laid by aligning a white line painted along the top of the barrel, with the target or aiming mark and the barrel raised or lowered to the correct elevation. Maximum range for any charge is achieved with the barrel at an angle of 45°.

The Hotchkiss-Brandt 60mm Commando mortar (controlled firing model).

9mm Walther P1 Pistol

Germany (FGR)

Calibre: 9mm
Length: 21.8cm
Length of barrel: 12.4cm
Weight: .96kg (loaded)
Mag capacity: 8 rounds
Muzzle velocity: 360m/s
Max effective range: 50m

The P1 is the modern version of the wartime Walther P38 which was the standard Wehrmacht pistol — numbers of these weapons manufactured before

1945 remain in use with various nations around the world (eg Yugoslavia). The P1 differs from the P38 in having a lighter receiver and a different firing pin. It is the standard service pistol of West Germany, Norway, Portugal and Chile and is a popular weapon with many police forces. It is also manufactured in Austria by Steyr-Daimler-Puch AG.

The Walther 9mm P1 pistol.

7.65mm Walther PP and PPK Pistol   Germany (FGR)

Data: Model PP
Calibre: 7.65mm and 9mm
Length: 17.3cm
Length of barrel: 9.9cm
Weight: .682kg
Mag capacity: 8 rounds (PPK 7 rounds)
Muzzle velocity: 290m/s (7.65mm)
Max effective range: 40m

The PP first appeared in 1929 and ever since has been a popular pistol for both police and military duties. It remains in service with Hungary and Guyana both as a service arm and as a military police pistol. It is made in Turkey where it is known as the MKE Kirikkale and until several years ago was licence-made by Manuhrin in France. The PPK is a smaller 'pocket' pistol using the same basic mechanism which is still used by many police and service arms. The Hungarians call it the 7.65mm and M48 pistol.

Right: The 7.65mm PP pistol which is made in Germany by Carl Walther of Ulm.

9mm Walther PP-SUPER Pistol   Germany (FGR)

Calibre: 9mm
Length: 176mm
Length of barrel: 92mm
Weight: .85kg (loaded)
Mag capacity: 7 rounds
Muzzle velocity: 325m/s
Max effective range: 40m

The Walther PP-SUPER is a thoroughly updated version of the Walther PP pistol and it is chambered for the 9mm × 18mm cartridge. It uses the same form of automatic safety mechanism as that used on the Walther P4 pistol but on the PP-SUPER the construction is entirely of steel. Apart from the safety, the basic PP mechanism and features are unchanged but a general restyle of the design has been made. Like the earlier PP, the PP-SUPER seems likely to be sold to many civil and military police forces.

9mm Walther P4 and P38K Pistol

	P4	P38K
Calibre	9mm	9mm
Length:	20cm	16cm
Length of barrel:	11cm	7cm
Weight (loaded):	.925kg	.89kg
Magazine capacity:	8 rounds	8 rounds
Muzzle velocity:	373m/s	320m/s
Maximum effective range:	50m	50m

The Walther P4 is an updating of the basic Walther P1(P38) pistol which incorporates the latest Walther safety devices. One of these is that the hammer can be lowered without firing a chambered round by deflecting the firing pin downwards with a side-mounted spring-loaded lever. Once lowered the pin cannot reach the base of the round unless the trigger is deliberately pulled. Thus the need for a manual

Walther 9mm P4 pistol.

safety is eliminated. All the other features of the modern P1 are retained, but a new version, the P38K, has a shortened barrel with the fore sight mounted on the slide instead of over the muzzle. The P38K is intended for easy concealment, and may thus become a sidearm of considerable interest to many military and civilian police forces.

Right: Walther 9mm P38K pistol.

41

9mm Walther P5 Pistol

Calibre: 9mm
Length: 17.9cm
Length of barrel: 8.9cm
Weight: .96kg (loaded)
Mag capacity: 8 rounds (plus one round in chamber)
Muzzle velocity: 350-420m/s
Max effective range: 50m

The Walther P5 is an entirely new and modern pistol design which departs from previous Walther practice in having a rotating barrel locking system. Other features are the use of the new Walther safety mechanism as used on the PP-Super and P4 and the use of (optional) Betalights on the fore and rear sights for firing in poor visibility or darkness. The cartridge used is the well-tried 9mm × 19mm Parabellum.

Heckler and Koch Pistols

	VP70Z	VP70	P9S	P9	HK4
Calibre:	9mm	9mm	9mm or 7.65mm	9mm or 7.65mm	.38in/.32in/.25in/.22in
Length:	20.4cm	20.4cm	19.2cm	19.2cm	15.7cm
Length of barrel:	11.6cm	11.6cm	10.2cm	10.2cm	8.5cm
Weight (empty):	0.82kg	0.82kg	0.85kg	0.85kg	0.45kg
Weight (loaded):	1.14kg	1.14kg	1.03/1.0kg	1.03/1.0kg	0.59/0.58/0.56/0.55kg
Magazine capacity:	18	18	9/8	9/8	7/8/8/8
Muzzle velocity:	360m/s	360m/s	350/370m/s	350/370m/s	290/250/240/250m/s

VP70Z

This automatic pistol is recoil operated with an inertia bolt and a stationary barrel. The parallely guided revolver trigger (double action only) and the direct firing pin ignition ensure constant readiness to fire and permit the weapon to be carried while loaded and uncocked until the trigger is pulled.

VP70

A holster stock, containing a three round burst device, converts the VP70 pistol into a compact SMG. Bursts are only possible in conjunction with this holster stock.

The Heckler and Koch 9mm VP70 pistol complete with holster stock.

The Heckler and Koch P9S pistol.

P9S

This high performance automatic pistol is characterised by the polygon profile of the barrel interior and the roller locking action. The distribution of the momentum in the bolt, reduces the recoil velocity of the slide significantly, and with it the noticeable kick.

P9

This is similar to the P9S except that it provides a shorter trigger reach as well as a trigger stop, and has a single action trigger.

HK4

This pistol can be fitted with any one of four barrels after simple adjustments have been carried out. The trigger is of the double action type and the loaded weapon may therefore by carried safely.

9mm M1908 Pistol

Germany

Calibre: 9mm
Length: 22cm
Length of barrel: 10cm
Weight: .988kg (loaded)
.89kg (empty)
Mag capacity: 8 rounds
Muzzle velocity: 322m/s
Effective range: 50m

This is the world-famous Luger pistol. The first model entered production in 1898 in 7.65mm calibre. Later models came in 1900, 1902, 1904 and 1908, but the Luger was supplemented in the German Army from 1938 by the Walther P38. The weapon is still in service in many countries and is now being manufactured for commercial sales by Mauser-Werke GmbH of Oberndorf, West Germany. Its method of operation is of the short recoil type and it fires the 9mm Parabellum round.

It is recognisable by its distinctive and unique toggle-locking system with two milled knobs on the top of the receiver, a square plate above the trigger on the LHS, and a semi-circular recess cut in the bottom of the grip to receive the circular magazine button.

The fore sight is of the blade type and the rear sight is of the open V-notch type.

9mm Heckler and Koch MP5 Sub-Machine Gun

Germany (FGR)

Data: MP5A2
Calibre: 9mm
Length: 68cm
Length of barrel: 22.5cm
Weight: 2.94kg (loaded)
Mag capacity: 10.15 or 30 rounds
Muzzle velocity: 400m/s

Max effective range: 200-300m
Rate of fire: 650rmp (cyclic)
100rpm (auto)
50rpm (single shot)

The Heckler and Koch 9mm MP5A2 SMG with special sight.

The MP5 was at one time known as the HK54 and it is a shortened version of the Heckler and Koch G3 rifle with which is shares many interchangeable components. The basic MP5 is fitted with a fixed plastic stock as the MP5A2 while the MP5A3 has a sliding metal stock. Both versions can be fitted with a .22in cub-calibre training device. The MP5 SD is a silenced version and is available without a stock as the MP5 SD 1, with a stock as the MP5 SD 2 and with a sliding metal stock as the MP5 SD 3. The latest model in the series is the MP5K which has been developed for police and anti-terrorist squads. This model weighs only 2kg and is 32.5cm long. It is basically the MP5 without a stock, a shorter barrel

The Heckler and Koch 9mm MP5A3 SMG with sliding metal stock.

(11.5cm long) and a small handgrip mounted forward of the magazine. In all its forms the MP5 is regarded as one of the most accurate SMGs available and accuracy is improved on some recent production versions by the fitting of a mechanism that restricts bursts to three rounds on automatic. All the MP5 weapons make extensive use of nylon and plastic furniture and steel stampings. They are used by German Police and para-military units, and some have been sold to small armies abroad.

The Heckler and Koch 9mm MP5 SD 2 silenced SMG with fixed stock.

The Heckler and Koch 9mm MP5K SMG for police and anti-terrorist squads.

9mm Walther MP-L and MP-K Sub-Machine Guns

Germany (FGR)

Data: MP-K
Calibre: 9mm
Length: 65.3cm (stock extended)
36.8cm (stock folded)
Length of barrel: 17.1cm
Weight: 3.425kg (loaded)
Mag capacity: 32 rounds
Muzzle velocity: 356m/s
Max effective range: 200m
Rate of fire: 550rpm

The Walther MP-L and MP-K differ only in the length of barrel fitted with the -L version having the longer barrel. Both were first produced in 1963 and were procured for police and naval units in Germany.

The Walther MP-L SMG (top) and Walther MP-K SMG (above); both weapons have their stocks folded.

9mm MP40 Sub-Machine Gun

Germany (FGR)

Calibre: 9mm
Length: 83.3cm (stock extended)
63cm (stock folded)
Length of barrel: 25.1cm
Weight: 4.7kg (loaded)
Mag capacity: 32 rounds
Muzzle velocity: 381m/s
Max effective range: 200m
Rate of fire: 500rpm (cyclic)

The MP40 was developed from the MP38 and MP38/40 and during the war it was produced in very large numbers. After 1945 it remained in service with many nations but today it is used by very few armed forces. Norway is one exception where the MP40 is called the Maskin 9mm M40. The MP40 is still a popular weapon with many irregular and guerrilla organisations and has been encountered in Vietnam and in various African states.

4.6mm Heckler and Koch HK36 Assault Rifle
Germany (FGR)

Calibre: 4.6mm
Length: 88.9cm (butt extended)
76.9cm (butt retracted)
Length of barrel: 38.1cm
Weight: 3.67kg (with 90 rounds)
2.849kg (empty)
Mag capacity: 30 or 90 rounds
Range: 300m
Rate of fire: 1,100/1,200rpm (cyclic)
90/180rpm (practical)

The HK36 assault rifle has been designed by Heckler and Koch. Although it has been tested by the German Army it is not yet in production.

The weapon fires a 4.6mm × 36mm round. Two types of cartridge have been developed, one with a conventional lead core (m/v 850m/s) and the other with a tungsten-carbide core (m/v 777m/s). It is recoil-operated and its bolt system is of the delayed roller locked type. The selector is on the left side and the settings are for safe, single shots and full automatic, the latter giving controlled bursts of 2-5 rounds. The HK36 has a reflex sight with daylight screen and a betalight for twilight operations.

The main advantage of the weapon is its light weight. For example the HK36 assault rifle with 500 rounds is equivalent to a standard German Army 7.62mm G3 rifle with 100 rounds of ammunition. The 4.6mm ammunition has greater penetration performance and an asymmetrical point.

The 4.6mm HK36 assault rifle.

5.56mm Heckler and Koch HK33 Rifle
Germany (FGR)

Calibre: 5.56mm
Length: 92cm (butt stock)
75.5cm (retracted stock)
67cm (carbine, retracted stock)
Length of barrel: 39cm
32.2cm (carbine)
Weight: 3.35kg (HK33A2)
Mag capacity: 20 or 40 rounds

Muzzle velocity: 920m/s
Max effective range: 400m
Rate of fire: 600-650rpm (cyclic)
100rpm (auto)
40rpm (single shots)

The Heckler and Koch HK33A2 rifle.

The HK33 is a member of the Heckler and Koch Group 2 family of weapons — Group 1 firing the NATO 7.62mm round and Group 3 firing the Russian 7.62mm round. Group 2 weapons all fire the American 5.56mm × 45mm round and the HK33 can be fitted with a 20 or 40-round magazine. The HK33A2 has a rigid buttstock and the HK33A3 uses a telescopic butt. The HK33A2 fitted with a telescopic sight is known as the HK33ZF. There is a carbine version with a telescopic stock known as the HK33KA1. The sniper's version is called the HK33 SG/1, this is provided with a bipod which folds up under the front of the weapon when not in use. The full range of Heckler and Koch accessories can be fitted to all versions except that the carbine version

The Heckler and Koch HK33A3 rifle.

cannot be used to fire the 40mm grenade. Although not selected for Bundeswehr use the HK33 is in limited production by GIAT in France and also made in Saudi Arabia. Malaysia has bought 5,000.

The Heckler and Koch Group 2 family of weapons is completed by the HK13 and HK23A1 machine guns and HK53 sub-machine gun, but none of these weapons has yet been adopted either. For firing from the ports of MICVs another model of the HK33 has been developed, this is called the HK33KL.

7.62mm Heckler and Koch G3 Rifle   Germany (FGR)

Calibre: 7.62mm
Length: 102cm (fixed butt)
Length of barrel: 45cm
Weight: 5kg (loaded)
Mag capacity: 20 rounds
Muzzle velocity: 780-800m/s
Max effective range: 400m
Rate of fire: 500-600rpm (cyclic)
100rpm (auto)
40rpm (single shots)

After 1945 a group of German designers produced the CETME automatic rifle in Spain, and the design was eventually produced by Heckler and Koch for the Bundeswehr as the Gewehr 3 or G3A3. The type has since been exported widely and produced under licence by a large number of countries. There are some variations to the basic design as one version has a retracting butt (G3A4), and, when fitted with a telescopic sight, it is known as the G3A3ZF. (Singlepoint sights can also be fitted.) There is a special sniper's version, the G3 SG/1, which differs in small details from the basic G3A3. Extensive use is made of plastic furniture and metal stamping in the design, and the G3 can be fitted with a bayonet, bipod, a sub-calibre training device, a 40mm muzzle-mounted grenade launcher and a special plastic blank round for training. Spain continues to produce the original version as the CETME Model 58.

The G3 rifle is a member of the Heckler and Koch Weapons System Group 1. This group of weapons is completed by the HK21A1 and HK11A1 machine guns. The former is fed from a link belt while the latter is fed from a 30-round box magazine.

Producer Countries
Brazil, France, Iran, Malaysia, Norway, Pakistan, Portugal, Saudi Arabia, Sweden, Thailand, Turkey, United Kingdom, West Germany.

User Countries
Abu Dhabi, Bangladesh, Bolivia, Brunei, Burma, Chad, Chile, Columbia, Denmark, Dominican Republic, Dubai, El Salvador, Ghana, Guyana, Haiti, Indonesia, Iran, Ivory Coast, Jordan, Kenya, Malawi, Malaysia, Niger, Nigeria, Peru, Philippines, Qatar, Saudi Arabia, Senegal, Sharjah, Sudan, Sweden, Switzerland, Tanzania, Thailand, Togo, Turkey, Uganda, Upper Volta, Zambia.

Above: The Heckler and Koch G3A3 rifle.

Below: Latest export version of the Heckler and Koch G3A3 has a different forestock than the G3A3 used by the German Army.

Above: The Heckler and Koch G3 SG/1 sniper's rifle with the bipod in the retracted position.

Below: The Heckler and Koch HK21A1 7.62mm belt-fed machine gun.

Above: *The Heckler and Koch G3A3ZF rifle with telescopic sights.*

Below: *The Heckler and Koch G3A4 rifle with retracting butt.*

7.92mm MP44 Assault Rifle   Germany

Calibre: 7.92mm
Length: 93.3cm (overall)
Length of barrel: 41.3cm
Weight: 5.2kg (loaded)
4.5kg (empty)
Mag capacity: 30 rounds
Muzzle velocity: 686m/s
Effective range: 400m (semi-auto)
200m (auto)
Rate of fire: 800rpm (cyclic)
100-120rpm (auto)
40-50rpm (semi-auto)

This weapon can be said to be the forerunner of the modern assault rifle. Design of an assault rifle (automatic) started in Germany in 1938 and two

companies built prototypes: Haenel, the MKb42 (H) and Carl Walther, the MKb42(W). The MKb42 (H) was modified and became the MP43 and later the MP44 (Sturmgewehr) and saw service in the last 18 months of World War II.

It is gas-operated and is capable of full and semi-automatic fire. Its front sight is of the hooded blade type and its rear sight is of the adjustable V-notch type. It fires the 7.92mm × 33mm cartridge.

The weapon is still used by a number of countries including the East German Workers' Militia.

The 7.92mm MP44 Assault Rifle

7.92mm Mauser Model 98 Rifle   Germany

Data: Kar98k
Calibre: 7.92mm
Length: 111cm
Length of barrel: 59.7cm
Weight: 3.9kg (empty)
Mag capacity: 5 rounds
Muzzle velocity: 754m/s
Max effective range: 600m (plus)

The Mauser Rifle has been in production since the 1880s in one form or another and it has the distinction of being produced in larger numbers than any other military rifle. Before and during World War II the standard Wehrmacht rifle was the Karabiner 1898k or Kar98k and this version was produced with minor variations by Czechoslovakia (vz24), Belgium, Spain and other nations. After 1945 the Kar98k remained in use with many nations such as Czechoslovakia (until 1952), Portugal (as the (937), Norway, Spain, Indonesia and Albania. It is still reportedly in service in Albania, Norway, Spain and Yugoslavia (as the Puska 7.9mm, M-48), and many central American states. A copy manufactured after the war in Taiwan is known as the 7.92mm Rifle Model Chiang Kai-shek and Israel is known to have re-calibred some Kar98ks to the 7.62mm NATO calibre. As a result of a large number of versions currently available on the second-hand market, this weapon is often encountered in the hands of irregular and guerrilla forces. There are many other types of Mauser rifle still in service, for example Mexico adopted the 7mm rifle in 1895 and other models were built in 1902, 1912 and 1936. The latter was similar in appearance to the American Springfield. The last model was the M1954 which was chambered for the American .30in cartridge.

The Mauser 7.92mm Model 98 rifle with telescopic sight.

7.62mm Heckler and Koch HK21 Machine Gun   Germany (FGR)

Calibre: 7.62mm
Length: 102.1cm (with butt)
82cm (without butt)
Length of barrel: 45cm
Weight: 7.92kg (with bipod)
Type of feed: 100-round belt or 20-round mag
Muzzle velocity: 800m/s
Max effective range: 1,200m
Rate of fire: 850rpm (cyclic)
200rpm (practical)

The HK21 uses a number of G3 rifle components and has the same basic mechanism. It has been designed to carry out a number of roles and can have either a magazine feed or a belt feed from the left. It can be fired from a bipod or a tripod and the butt can be removed for mounting on or in vehicles. The standard weapon fires the 7.62mm × 51mm NATO cartridge but by changing the barrel, bolt and bolt feed, the HK21 can fire the Russian 7.62mm × 39mm cartridge. A similar change can be made for the 5.56mm × 45mm round. A later version, the HK21A1, has a modified feed belt, and at the time of writing it seems likely that this version will be bought by Sweden. The HK21 is in service with the Portuguese Army and other armies in Africa and Asia and has not been accepted for Bundeswehr use. An LMG version, the HK11, is also in production.

7.62mm MG1 to MG3 Machine Guns   Germany (FGR)

Calibre: 7.62mm
Length: 122.5cm
Length of barrel: 53.1cm
Weight: 11.5kg (with bipod)
Type of feed: Belt
Muzzle velocity: 820m/s
Max effective range: 800m (on bipod)
Rate of fire: 700-1,300rpm (cyclic)
250rpm (auto)

When the 7.92mm MG42 entered service with the Wehrmacht in late 1942 it revolutionised machine gun design not only by its very efficient mechanism but by its construction which involved a maximum number of steel pressings and a minimum of costly machining processes. It also offered a fast barrel change. After the war the design was resurrected by Rheinmetall in the 7.62mm × 51mm NATO calibre and in this form was offered commercially as the MG42/59. It was taken into Bundeswehr service as the MG1 and there were sub-variants such as the MG1A1, MG1A2, MG1A3, MG1A4 and MG1A5. These sub-variants had changes to the feed mechanism, muzzle booster and mountings. The MG2 was a conversion of war-production MG42s to the 7.62mm calibre. The MG3 is the latest version

and has a number of changes, especially to the feed which can now cope with a wide range of ammunition belt eg the cartridge belt DM-1, disintegrating belts DN-13/3 and the American M-13. The MG3 can be used on a bipod or tripod and can be fitted as a coaxial vehicle weapon as the MG3A1. A wide range of accessories can be used and special AA mounts are available. A new version of the MG3 is the MG3e which uses various alloy sub-assemblies to reduce the weight by 2.2kg. Despite this weight reduction the new model is fully interchangeable with all existing accessories and part interchangeability with parts from the normal MG3 is 'guaranteed'. The MG3 is also produced in Italy, Spain, Pakistan and Portugal. It is used by the armed forces of West Germany, Austria (MG42/59), Denmark (designated MG62), Chile (MG42/59), Turkey, Norway (MG3), Iran (MG1A1) and the Sudan. The original MG42 is still encountered in the hands of irregular and guerrilla forces while the SARAC M53 is a Yugoslav version of the MG42 which is still produced in that country in the original 7.92mm and this version is virtually identical to the original.

A MG42 on tripod.

Above: The MG3 machine gun showing bipod and ammunition feed.

Below: MG3 machine gun team of the German Army.

7.92mm MG34 Machine Gun   Germany

Calibre: 7.92mm
Length: 122.4cm
Length of barrel: 62.9cm
Weight: 35kg (tripod)
11.5kg (bipod)
Type of feed: 75-round drum
50-round belt
Muzzle velocity: 755m/s
Max effective range: 600m (on bipod)
1,800-2,000m (on tripod)
Rate of fire: 800-900rpm (cyclic)
300rpm (practical on tripod)
120rpm (practical on bipod)

The MG34 was one of the two standard machine guns of the Wehrmacht during World War II. It is no longer in front-line use anywhere but some are still used by the East German Militia and it forms the primary armament of the East German SK-1 Armoured Car which is used by para-military units. Some were reported to have been seen in action in Vietnam and Angola and a few were observed in the

street fighting in Beirut in early 1976. The 7.92mm
MG13 machine gun was seen in action during the
Angolan war of early 1976.

The 7.92mm MG34 machine gun.

Armbrust 300 Anti-Tank Weapon Germany (FGR)

Calibre: 80mm
Weight: 6.3kg
Length: 85cm
Range: 300m
Crew: 1

The Armbrust 300 has been developed to prototype stage by Messerschmitt-Bolköw-Blohm of Otto-brunn and has been tested both in Germany and the United States.

The Armbrust has the following features—no firing report, no muzzle flash, no rear blast or flash or smoke. Its HEAT round will penetrate 300mm of armour plate and has a m/v of 220m/s, time to 300m is 1.5sec. The round is not armed until it is 7-12m from the weapon. Once fired Armbrust is discarded. An illuminating round with a range of 1,000m is available as is a fragmentation round with a range of 500m.

The Armbrust consists of the sight, pistol trigger mechanism with cocking lever and safety, shoulder rest for firing in the standing of kneeling position, shoulder butt for firing in the prone position cheek protector and carrying handle and strap.

Panzerfaust 44 Anti-Tank Weapon — Germany (FGR)

Calibre: 44mm
Weight: 7.8kg
Length: 118cm (loaded)
88cm (empty)
Range: 200m (old round)
400m (new round)
Crew: 1

	Old Round	New Round
Calibre of rocket:	81mm	67mm
Initial velocity:	107m/s	168m/s
Max velocity:	107m/s	210m/s
Max range:	200m	400m
Armour penetration:	32cm	37cm

The PZF 44 is the standard light anti-tank weapon of the German Army and is believed to be in service with a number of other NATO countires. It is of the reusable type and can be quickly reloaded. The original round has been replaced by a new round which has been developed by Dynamit Nobel AG. Basic data of the two rounds is shown above.

Panzerfaust 44 anti-tank weapon without the fin-stabilised rocket in position.

40mm Heckler and Koch HK69A1 Grenade Germany (FGR) Launcher

Calibre: 40mm
Length: 61cm (butt extended)
43cm (butt retracted)
Weight: 2.03kg (loaded)
1.8kg (empty)
.23kg (weight of grenade)

Muzzle velocity: 75m/s
Range: 350m (max)

The HK69A1 is a single-shot, break-action weapon with a retractable buttstock, fixed fore sight and a folding ladder pattern rear sight. It is intended to bridge the gap between the maximum hand grenade throwing range and the minimum range of a mortar. The grenades are effective against light armoured vehicles and personnel. The fore sight is of the fixed barleycorn type while the rear sight is fixed for

Heckler and Koch HK69A1 40mm grenade launcher with butt retracted and rear sight folded down.

targets up to 100m, the folding ladder type sight being graduated for 150, 200, 250, 300 and 350m.

.38in No 2 Pistol Revolver Great Britain

Calibre: .38in (9.65mm)
Length: 26cm
Length of barrel: 12.7cm
Weight: .767kg
Cylinder capacity: 6 rounds
Muzzle velocity: 183m/s
Max effective range: 30m

Developed from the earlier .38in Webley Mk IV pistol, the .38in No 2 Pistol Revolver is often referred to as the 'Enfield'. It is no longer in service with the British forces but is still used by many UK police forces and remains in service in New Zealand, Cyprus, and many other Commonwealth and ex-Commonwealth armies and police forces. There are two main versions, the No 2 Mk 1, and the No 2 Mk 1* which has a double-action only trigger mechanism and thus lacks a hammer thumb notch.

The .38 No 2 Mk 1 revolver.

.455in Webley Pistol

Great Britain

Calibre: .455in (11.6mm) (nominal)
.441in (11.2mm) (actual)
Length: 28.6cm
Length of barrel: 15.2cm
Weight: 1.07kg (empty)
Cylinder capacity: 6 rounds
Muzzle velocity: 183m/s
Max effective range: 50m

The first Webley .455in pistol entered service in 1887 and since that time has been produced in large numbers in a variety of marks and with different barrel lengths. The last service mark was the Pistol, Webley, 6in barrel, Mk 6 which entered service in 1915 and it was declared obsolete by the British Army in 1947 by which time it was known as the Pistol Revolver .455in No 1 Mk 6. Despite its age it is still in use all over the world as its massive and heavy construction ensures that it will take a long time to wear out and the large calibre bullet is very useful for close-quarter fighting. The Webley .455in is still likely to be encountered in such countries as Egypt and Jordan, and it remains in service with many British-trained armies and police forces.

The .455in Webley pistol.

9mm Sterling Mk 4 (L2A3) Sub-Machine Gun

Great Britain

Calibre: 9mm
Length: 69cm (butt extended)
48.2cm (butt folded)
Length of barrel: 19.8cm
Weight: 3.47kg (loaded)
Mag capacity: 34 rounds
Muzzle velocity: 390m/s
Range: 200m
Rate of fire: 550rmp (cyclic)

Adopted for British Forces use in 1954 (as the L3A4) the Sterling has been sold to well over 70 military and defence forces throughout the world. Developed from the earlier Patchett SMG, the Sterling can be fitted with a bayonet and it is a reliable and efficient weapon under a wide range of conditions. Single-shot fire can be selected, and the sights have two range settings — 100m and 200m. This weapon is also manufactured in Canada (as the C1) and in India.

Above: The Sterling SMG with butt folded.

Below: The Sterling SMG with butt extended.

9mm Sterling Patchett Mk 5 (L34A1) Silenced Sub-Machine Gun

Great Britain

Calibre: 9mm
Length: 85.7cm (butt extended)
65.4cm (butt folded)
Length of barrel: 19.8cm
Weight: 4.25kg (loaded)
Mag capacity: 34 rounds
Muzzle velocity: 308m/s
Max effective range: 150m
Rate of fire: 515-565rpm (cyclic)
402rpm (practical)

The Mk 5 Sterling was designed to a British General Staff specification which called for a weapon that

when fired would be inaudible at 30m and unrecognisable as a firearm when fired at a range of 50m. The Mk 5 is basically a Sterling Mk 4 with an advanced design of silencer added and mechanically the two marks are identical. In use the weapon would be fired using aimed single shots only, with the automatic fire mode being used only as an emergency extra. The Scotos night sight can be fitted as an extra.

Sten Guns   Great Britain

Data: Mk 11
Calibre: 9mm
Length: 76.2cm
Length of barrel: 19.7cm
Weight: 3.44kg (loaded)
2.8kg (empty)
Mag capacity: 32 rounds
Muzzle velocity: 366m/s
Max effective range: 200m
Rate of fire: 540rpm

The Sten was first produced in 1940 and was designed for easy manufacture at low cost. It was produced in a variety of marks, the most numerous of

which was the Mk 11 and over 2,000,000 were made. Other marks featured silencers and such extras as wooden butts and foregrips. Although now withdrawn from use in most front-line forces throughout the world, the Sten is still in use with some police forces and military units, both regular and irregular.

The 9mm Sten SMG.

4.85mm Individual Weapon   Great Britain

Calibre: 4.85mm
Length: 77cm
Length of barrel: 51.85cm
Weight: 4.12kg (loaded)
Mag capacity: 20 rounds
Muzzle velocity: 900m/s
Rate of fire: 700-850rpm (cyclic)

The British submission for a new standard NATO calibre has been under development since about 1970, and the resultant calibre selection of 4.85mm

(.191in) has been arrived at after a long series of trials. The weapon to fire the new round, the 4.85mm Individual Weapon has been developed by the Royal Small Arms Factory, Enfield. This weapon is fitted with an advanced optical sight, a small bayonet and can fire grenades. A night sight is under development. The Individual Weapon is conventionally gas-operated and uses a rotary forward locking bolt. Weight of a 4.85mm round is 11.6g.

The new personal 4.85mm weapon with its distinctive optical sight is made even more unusual by its lack of orthodox butt which allows the weapon to use a barrel of suitable length while being much shorter over all.

7.62mm Parker-Hale Model 82 Rifle Great Britain

Parker-Hale Model 82 rifle with telescopic sight.

Calibre: 7.62mm
Length: 121.3cm (max)
116.2cm (min)
Length of barrel: 66cm
Weight: 4.8kg
Mag capacity: 4 rounds
Max range: Dependent on user's skill

In August 1978 the Australian Army announced that after some years of exhaustive trials they had decided to adopt the Parker-Hale Model 82 firing 7.62mm NATO ammunition as their new sniper rifle. The Model 82 is basically a target rifle adapted to the more robust needs of the military but retaining the high manufacturing standards that Parker-Hale have

long been renowned for. The barrel is cold forged and carefully treated to retain maximum accuracy, and the fittings have several features to allow the individual to alter the rifle to suit his physical requirements. One is the use of removable butt sections and another is the movable front sling stop. The bolt action is that of the Mauser Model 98 but high standards of construction and machining have been incorpoated. The Model 82 has an unusual trigger lock which not only acts as a normal safety, but also acts as a trigger lock and bolt lock. The telescopic sight matched to the Model 82 in Australian Army use is the Kahles-Helia ZF69.

7.62mm L42A1 Rifle Great Britain

Calibre: 7.62mm
Length: 118.1cm
Length of barrel: 69.9cm
Weight: 4.43kg

Mag capacity: 10 rounds
Muzzle velocity: 838m/s
Range: 800-1,000m

The L42A1 is a version of the 7.62mm L39A1 intended for service use by snipers. (The L39A1 is not intended primarily as a service rifle but is intended for competition use by Army units, and differs from the L42A1 in many details.) Basically, the L42A1 is a conversion of the No 4 Mk 1 (T) rifles to take 7.62mm ammunition. A L1A1 sighting telescope is fitted as standard, but fixed sights are still incorporated.

The 7.62mm L42A1 sniper's rifle with telescopic sight.

.303in No 5 Mk 1 Rifle

Great Britain

Calibre: .303in (7.7mm)
Length: 100.3cm
Length of barrel: 47.6cm
Weight: 3.24kg
Mag capacity: 10 rounds
Max effective range: 400m

Designed in 1943 the No 5 Mk 1 was a shortened version of the No 4 intended for use in the jungles of the Far East. It was fitted with a flash hider and, as recoil was rather heavy, a rubber butt pad was also standard. Now out of service with British forces the No 5 remains in use with some Asian and African states.

.303in No 4 Mk 1 Rifle

Great Britain

Calibre: .303in (7.7mm)
Length: 112.85cm
Length of barrel: 64cm
Weight: 4kg
Mag capacity: 10 rounds
Muzzle velocity: 751m/s
Range: Sighted up to 1,300yd (1,280m)

The No 4 Mk 1 was approved for production in November 1939 after trials had taken place as far back as 1926. The new rifle was designed for mass production and differed from the earlier No 1 rifles in having part of the barrel protruding from the front of the stock. The sights and trigger mechanism were also revised. The No 4 was produced in millions in the UK and in Canada, the USA and India. After extensive use during World War II and since, the No 4 is no longer in front-line service with British Forces but it remains in use with some TAVR units and the Ulster Defence Regiment. Overseas is is still in front-line use with Middle East and Asian armies, and large number have been converted for sporting purposes. The No 4 can be fitted with a spike or blade bayonet, and is also used to fire a variety of grenades. There are a number of sub-variants such as the No 4 Mk 1*, the Mk 2, the Mk 1/2 and 1/3, none of which differ from the original mark except in minor manufacturing detail.

The No 4 Mk 1 rifle is still regarded as one of the finest military rifles ever produced.

Some No 4 Mk 1 rifles have been rebored to the standard 7.62mm calibre and in this form are known as the L8A4. Both these and the .303in versions can be fitted with telescopic sights (eg: Rifle No 4 Mk 1 (T) and Mk 1* (T)).

The Rifle No 4 Mk 1.

.303in No 1 SMLE Mk 111* Rifle   Great Britain

Calibre: .303in (7.7mm)
Length: 113cm
Length of barrel: 64cm
Weight: 3.91kg
Mag capacity: 10 rounds
Muzzle velocity: 744m/s
Effective range: Up to 1,000m

The Rifle No 1 Mk 111* was first manufactured in 1916 and was a simplified version of the No 1 Mk 111. To ease production the Mk 111* did not have a magazine cut-off and the sights were simpler. The Mk 111* was produced in large quantities both in the UK and India, and the Mk 111* remained in production in Australia until 1955 (the Australian Army did not adopt the later No 4 rifle). Over the years the No 1 Mk 111* was produced with some minor variation and as the type was essentially a hand-built weapon, some variation on the above dimensions may occur. In 1975 the Mk 111* is still in widespread use in the Middle East and India and its robust and reliable construction will ensure a long life for it yet.

Rifle No 1 SMLE Mk III.*

4.85mm Light Support Weapon   Great Britain

Calibre: 4.85mm
Length: 90cm
Length of barrel: 64.6cm
Weight: 5.26kg (loaded)
Mag capacity: 20 or 30 rounds
Muzzle velocity: 930m/s
Rate of fire: 700-850rpm (cyclic)

Developed by the Royal Small Arms Factory, Enfield, the Light Support Weapon (LSW) uses 80% of the components used on the Individual Weapon. The main changes are to the barrel, which is longer and a bipod is a permanent fixture. Normally a 30-round magazine is used but the Individual Weapon's 20-round magazine can also be used. Considerably lighter than the 7.62mm GPMG it is intended to replace, the LSW will probably be issued to infantry units at the rate of one LSW to every three Individual Weapons.

The 4.85mm infantry machine gun, properly known as the Light Support Weapon, is very similar to the personal weapon and shares many of its components. The obvious exterior differences are the longer barrel, larger magazines and bipod.

7.62mm L4A4 Light Machine Gun   Great Britain

The 7.62mm LMG L4A4.

Calibre: 7.62mm
Length: 113.3cm
Length of barrel: 53.6cm
Weight of gun: 9.5kg
Mag capacity: 20 or 30 rounds
Muzzle velocity: 823m/s
Max effective range: 800m
Rate of fire: 500rpm (cyclic)

The L4A4 is a conversion of the World War II .303in Bren Gun and so many conversions have been made over the years that it is very unlikely that any .303in Bren Guns remain in use anywhere (some 7.92mm versions produced in Canada during World War II may be encountered in the Far East, especially in China). Despite the 7.62mm conversion, the basic gas-operated mechanism of the Czech-designed Bren remains unchanged. Although no longer in front-line use with the British Army the L4A4 equips many units of the TAVR and is fitted to many vehicles as an AA weapon. Overseas, the L4A4 is in use in Australia and Malaysia, and in many other Commonwealth countries.

The L4A5 is a variant used by the Royal Navy.

The standard .303in Bren LMG.

7.62mm L7A2 General Purpose Machine Gun

Great Britain

Calibre: 7.62mm
Length: 123.2cm (as LMG)
Length of barrel: 62.8cm
Weight: 10.9kg
13.64kg (weight of L4A1 tripod)
Type of feed: 100 rounds in linked belt
Muzzle velocity: 838m/s
Range: Up to 1,800m
Rate of fire: 750-1,000rpm (cyclic)
LMG — up to 100rpm
Sustained fire on tripod — up to 200rpm

The L7A2 is the version of the Belgian FN MAG machine gun adopted for use by the British Army and it differs from the original in several respects. Most of these changes have been designed at Enfield and outwardly the gun is identical with the Belgian MAG. The L7A2 is usually known as the GPMG and it can be used as a LMG on a bipod or as a sustained fire weapon on a tripod. In this latter role a dial sight (the same as that used on the 81mm mortar) can be used for indirect firing.

The L8A1 is a variant designed for use on the Chieftain tank and a further variant is the L43A1 intended for use on the Scorpion light tank as a ranging machine gun. The L8A1 is designed for use as a normal MG in the ground role as is the L37A1 fitted to a variety of light AFVs.

The L20A1 is a variant for use on helicopters and aircraft machine gun pods.

Below: GPMG for use in the sustained fire role with tripod

Bottom: 7.62mm GPMG with bipod.

.303in Vickers Machine Gun

Great Britain

Calibre: .303in (7.7mm)
Length: 115.6cm
Length of barrel: 72.4cm
Weight: 15kg (without water)
18.2kg (with water)
22.7kg (weight of tripod)
Type of feed: 250-round belt
Muzzle velocity: 744m/s
Range: 4,117m (max, with Mk 8Z round)
Rate of fire: 450-500rpm

The Vickers machine gun was a development of the basic Maxim machine gun introduced into service as the Mk 1 in 1912. Despite the introduction of various marks for such uses as AFV installations, the basic design remained unchanged until its withdrawal from service with the British Army in 1968. However, it remains in service with some Middle and Far East forces (eg Arab Emirates and Pakistan) where its rugged and reliable construction continues to be appreciated. Its main disadvantage is its great weight, but with the Mark 8Z round it can be used at ranges of up to 4,117m and is fitted with a dial sight for indirect fire.

51mm Mortar

Great Britain

Calibre: 51mm
Length: 51.5cm
Weight: 4.6kg (complete)
.852kg (weight of bomb)
Range: 200m (min)
800m (max)

The 51mm Mortar has been designed to replace the elderly 2in Mortar (cf) in service with the British Army and is a simple weapon with a minimum of design complexities. The sight is a bubble device and elevation is altered by a telescopic monopod leg. For minimum ranges an insert with a long firing pin is fitted inside the barrel to shorted its effective length. The HE bomb is of advanced design and is constructed with a number of pre-formed fragments around the HE filling.

51mm mortar with monopod leg.

2in ML Mortar

Great Britain

Data: Mks 7* and 8
Calibre: 2.015in (51.18mm)
Length: 35.6cm (complete)
Weight: 3.3kg (complete)
1.022kg (HE bomb)
.909kg (smoke bomb)
.511kg (signal bomb)
Max range: 500m

The 2in Mortar originated before World War II and since 1945 has been used only for smoke and signal firing (the HE round was reintroduced for a short time

65

during the Borneo campaign). Although it was produced in a wide range of marks and submarks only the Mks 7* and 8, both with spade baseplates, remain in use. Sighting for both is a simple white line painted on the barrel. The 2in mortar is due for replacement by the 51mm mortar in the near future.

The 2in mortar remains in service in Pakistan and Denmark (as the 51mm M/45 Fa mortar).

The ML 2in mortar in action.

9mm PA-63 Pistol   Hungary

Calibre: 9mm
Length: 17.5cm
Length of barrel: 8.9cm
Weight: .665kg (loaded)
.597kg (empty)
Mag capacity: 7 rounds
Range: 50m

The PA-63 is a commercial weapon and is used by the Hungarian Armed Forces. It fires a 9mm cartridge with a m/v of 315m/s.

Other Hungarian Pistols

The 7.62mm Model 48 is essentially a copy of the German Walther PP pistol and is used by the Hungarian Police. It is a double-action blowback-operated weapon.

7.62mm Model 48 (48M) is the Hungarian model of the Soviet TT-33 pistol. It differs from the Soviet weapon in that it has vertical cuts on the slide, its grip markings consist of a star, wheatsheaf and hammer, surrounded by a wreath. A 9mm model of the TT-33 has been built but this is not used in Hungary.

7.62mm AMD Sub-Machine Gun   Hungary

Calibre: 7.62mm
Length: 85.1cm (butt extended)
64.8cm (butt folded)
Length of barrel: 31.8cm
Weight: 3.27kg
Mag capacity: 30 rounds
Muzzle velocity: 700m/s
Range: 300m

Rate of fire: 600rpm (cyclic)
120rpm (auto)
40rpm (single shots)

The 7.62mm AMD SMG with stock folded.

The Hungarian AMD is a sub-machine gun based on the standard AKM assault rifle. It has the same breech mechanism but a shorter barrel, forward pistol grip and a large muzzle brake. The rear sight is graduated to 800m rather than the 1,000m of standard AKMs. The stock folds along the right side of the weapon when not required. The AMD cannot be fitted with a bayonet. It fires the same 7.62mm × 38mm cartridge as the AKM but with a slightly lower muzzle velocity.

9mm Uzi Sub-Machine Gun Israel

The 9mm Uzi SMG with folding metal stock.

Calibre: 9mm
Length: 64cm (wood stock)
64cm (metal stock extended)
47cm (metal stock folded)
Length of barrel: 25.9cm
Weight: 4.13kg (loaded)
3.6kg (empty)
Mag capacity: 25, 32 or 64 rounds
Muzzle velocity: 400m/s
Max effective range: 200m
Rate of fire: 550-600rpm (cyclic)
128rpm (auto)
64rpm (single shot)

The Uzi sub-machine gun was designed in 1949 by Major Uzi Gal of the Israeli Army and it embodies a number of features taken from experimental Czech and other designs to form a very useful and sturdy weapon. One of the main design features of the Uzi is that its short length brought about by the use of a bolt that extends forward over the barrel, and the magazine housing is in the pistol grip. The gun is fired as the bolt travels forward so that the blowback bolt is lighter than the conventional equivalent. Manufacture has been simplified by the use of metal stampings and heat-resistant plastics. One useful feature for the soldier is that the magazines have viewing holes in their sides to that the magazine contents can be seen at a glance. The stock can be easily changed from a conventional wooden butt to a folding metal stock and a number of other accessories can be fitted. These include a bayonet, searchlight, grenade launcher and blank firing device. A special clip is used to join two magazines together in a 'L' configuration. The Uzi is manufactured by Israeli Military Industries for the Israeli Army and is licence-built by the Belgian FN concern for the Bundeswehr, where it is used as the MP-2. Other user nations are Iran, Venezuela and Thailand.

5.56mm Galil ARM Assault Rifle Israel

Calibre: 5.56mm
Length: 97.9cm (85.1cm) (stock extended)
74.2cm (61.4cm) (stock folded)
Length of barrel: 46cm (33cm)
Weight: 4.3kg with bipod and handle)
3.9kg (3.65kg) (basic)

5.01kg (4.21kg) (loaded with 35 rounds)
Mag capacity: 12, 35 or 50 rounds
Muzzle velocity: 980m/s (920m/s)
Max effective range: 600m (400m)

Data in brackets refers to Galil SAR

Rate of fire: 650rpm (cyclic)
105rpm (auto)
40rpm (single shots)

The 5.56mm Galil ARM assault rifle.

After the 1967 Six-Day War a series of trials were carried out by the Israeli Army to find an infantry weapon that could replace its existing range of rifles, sub-machine guns and light machine guns. In 1972 it chose the Galil assault rifle and production began in time for the first examples to be issued in 1974 and 1975. The Galil is an Israeli product based on the Finnish M62 which in its turn is a derivation of the Russian AK-47 assault rifle. There are three basic weapons in the range. The ARM (assault rifle/light machine gun) equipped with folding metal stock, bipod and carrying handle. The AR (assault rifle) equipped with folding metal stock but without bipod and carrying handle. The SAR (short assault rifle)

with shortened barrel and folding stock but without bipod and carrying handle. The Galil has several unusual features not the least of which is the fixed bipod that can be used as a wire-cutter. The operating handle, fire-selector and magazine catch can be used from either side of the weapon to ease handling by left- and right-handed people. All versions can be fitted with a bayonet, a plastic or wooden stock, blank firing attachment and both can be fitted with the 12-round magazine loaded with ballistite cartridges for firing grenades. The Dutch company of NWM has a licence to produce the Galil under the designation the MN 1.

The 5.56mm Galil SAR with folding butt.

52mm Mortar

Calibre: 52mm
Total weight: 7.9kg (with baseplate)
1.31kg (bipod only)
Length: 63.7cm (overall)
Length of barrel: 49cm
Range: 130m (min)
480m (max)
Crew: 2

Israel

This 52mm smooth-bore muzzle loaded mortar is manufactured by Israel Military Industries. The gunner holds the mortar with the baseplate on the ground and uses the white sight line on the barrel for aiming. The mortar is fired by turning the firing button at the base of the barrel. This weapon is employed by infantry units for plunging fire as well as direct fire from the prone position.

Three types of mortar bomb have been developed by Israel Military Industries for this weapon:

HE Round: Total weight is 1.02kg and it has a length of 25cm, main charge is 150g of TNT. M/v is 78m/s, max range of 460-480m at 45° angle of fire. Fitted with IMI no 161 fuse.

Smoke Round: Total weight is 92kg, 25cm long. Max range 400m, m/v 78m/s, smoke generates for approx 100sec. Time delay is 7.5sec.

Illuminating Round: Total weight is .8kg length 26cm. The parachute opens after 8sec at 350m range and a height of 100m illuminating power is 100,000 candelas, burns for approx 30sec.

The IMI 52mm mortar.

60mm Tampella Mortar

Israel

Calibre: 60.75mm
Weight: 14.5kg (total)
5.5kg (barrel and breech piece)
1.1kg (sight)
4.3kg (bipod)
3.4kg (baseplate)
Length of barrel: 74cm
Elevation: +40° to +79°
Traverse: 116° at 50° elevation
137° at 70° elevation
Range: 150m (min)
2.555m (max)
Crew: 2 (1 man can carry the complete weapon)

This smooth-bore muzzle-loaded weapon is manufactured by Soltam and can be used with or without the bipod. The barrel and breech are made of high tensile alloy steel. The baseplate is of welded construction and carries the breech piece ball socket in the centre. The bipod incorporates the elevating, traverse and divergence gear and is made of seamless steel tubes.

HE Bomb: Forged steel construction with a tail unit machined out of a single piece of extruded light metal. The charge system is so arranged the

The 60mm Tampella mortar.

secondaries cannot be ignited in a hot barrel. Weight is 1.541kg. The propellant system is made up of a primary charge and a combination of up to four secondary charges.

Smoke Bomb: Weight 1.541kg ballistic and propelling charges same as the HE bomb. Used both as a smoke bomb and as a ranging bomb and is filled with plastic phosphorous.

Beretta Model 81 (7.65mm) and 84 (9mm) Pistols — Italy

Model	81	84
Calibre:	7.65mm	9mm (short)
Length:	17.2cm	17.2cm
Length of barrel:	9.7cm	9.7cm
Weight with empty mag:	.665kg	.64kg
Mag capacity:	12 rounds	12 rounds

These two new Beretta pistols have the following features: semi-automatic operation, blow back action, exposed double action hammer, staggered magazine, chamber loaded indicator (when there is a round in the barrel the extractor protrudes laterally showing red, this allows the user to check visually whether there is a round in the barrel without having to retract the slide), disassembling device, reversible magazine release button, manual safety on both sides of the weapon and an option magazine safety which prevents the weapon firing when the magazine is removed, even if there is a cartridge in the chamber. The fore sight is of the blade type and is integral with the slide, the rear sight is a notched bar, dovetailed to the slide.

The Beretta Model 84 (9mm short) pistol with magazine to the right.

9mm Beretta Model 92 Pistol — Italy

Calibre: 9mm
Length: 21.7cm
Length of barrel: 12.5cm
Weight: .95kg (with empty mag)
Mag capacity: 15 rounds
Muzzle velocity: 390m/s

The Model 92 is the third member of a new family of pistols introduced by Beretta in 1976, the other two being the 7.65mm Model 81 and the similar 9mm Model 84. It employs a short recoil operating system and has a double-acting trigger mechanism. Its fore sight is of the blade type and is integral with the slide while the rear sight consists of a notched bar also dovetailed to the slide. The Model 92S is similar but has a modified safety mechanism mounted on the slide which provides a safe de-cocking facility. This has similar specifications to the Model 92 but has a weight of .98kg with an empty magazine.

The Beretta Model 92 9mm pistol with, on the right, the staggered magazine.

9mm Beretta Model 1951 Pistol

Italy

Calibre: 9mm
Length: 20.3cm
Length of barrel: 11.4cm
Weight: .89kg (empty-steel receiver)
.72kg (empty-aluminium receiver)
Mag capacity: 8 or 10 rounds (latter being a special mag)
Range: 50m
Rate of fire: 35rpm

The Beretta 9mm Model 1951 pistol is the standard pistol of the Italian Armed Forces and is also used by both Egypt and Israel. It is short recoil-operated and semi-automatic. It fires standard 9mm × 19mm Parabellum ammunition with a m/v of 350m/s. The fore sight is of the blade type and the rear sight of notch type.

71

9mm Beretta Model 1934 (Short) Pistol

Italy

Calibre: 9mm
Length: 15.2cm
Length of barrel: 8.9cm
Weight: .763kg (loaded)
.697kg (empty)
Mag capacity: 7
Range: 40m
Rate of fire: 28rpm

The Model 1934 is a development of an earlier Beretta design and is used by the Italian and Yugoslav Armies. It fires a short 9mm round with a m/v of 290m/s. It is blowback operated and semi-automatic. The fore sight is of the blade type and the rear sight is of the notch type.

9mm Beretta Model 12 Sub-Machine Gun

Italy

Calibre: 9mm
Length: 64.5cm (steel butt extended)
41.8cm (steel butt folded)
Length of barrel: 20cm
Weight: 3.4kg (wooden butt without mag)
3kg (steel butt without mag)
Mag capacity: 20, 30 or 40 rounds
Effective range: 200m
Rate of fire: 550rpm (cyclic)
120rpm (auto)
40rpm (single shots)

In the 1950s Beretta developed a number of SMGs as successors to the earlier MAB 38/49. The end result was the Model 12 which has been exported to a number of countries and has been built in Indonesia. Although some are used by special units of the Italian Army, their standard SMG remains the MAB 38/39.

System of operation is blowback and it fires standard 9mm Parabellum ammunition. The fore sight is of the blade type and the rear sight is of the flip type graduated for 100 and 200m.

It can fire either single shots or on full automatic, the selector being of the push through type. It is

The Beretta 9mm SMG Model 12S with folding metal stock extended.

available with either a wooden detachable butt or a steel folding butt.

The latest version is designated the Model 12S. This differs from the earlier Model 12 in the following points. New design of manual safety and fire selector, modified rear cap catch, front sight adjustable for elevation and windage, strengthened front and rear sight supports, new butt plate and an expoxy resin finish that is resistant to corrosion and wear. Weight with metal stock and without magazine is 3.2kg, length with stock folded 41.8cm, length with metal stock extended 66cm. Like the Model 12 it can be fitted with a detachable wooden butt or a steel folding butt.

9mm Beretta Model 38/49 (Model 4) Sub-Machine Gun   Italy

Calibre: 9mm
Length: 79cm
Length of barrel: 21cm
Weight: 4.64kg
3.89kg (without mag)
Mag capacity: 20 or 40 rounds
Max effective range: 200m
Rate of fire: 450/500rpm (cyclic)
120rpm (auto)
40rpm (single shots)

The Beretta MAB 38/49 (MAB = Moschetto Automatico Beretta) is a development of the earlier Model 38/44. The Model 4 has a manual safety catch whilst the Model 5 has an automatic safety catch. The front sight is of the blade type and the rear sight is of the U-notch type and set for 100m. The weapon has two triggers, the front one for single shots and the rear one for full automatic. It fires standard 9mm Parabellum ammunition.

The Model 38/49 (Models 4 and 5) is the standard SMG of the Italian Army and has been exported all over the world. It has also been built in Indonesia and a similar weapon is the San Cristobal SMG.

The 9mm Beretta SMG Model 38/49 (Model 5).

9mm Beretta Model M38/42 Sub-Machine Gun   Italy

Four models were developed and used during World War II and some of these remain in service today, for example in Romania and Yugoslavia. The M38/42 and M38/44 have no barrel jacket but use a lighter externally fluted barrel, their stock ending at the magazine. On the M38 and M38A however the stock ends half way down the barrel.

5.56mm Beretta Model 70 Rifle Family   Italy

	AR	SC	LMG
Calibre:	5.56mm	5.56mm	5.56mm
Length (with bayonet):	108cm	107.5cm	108cm
Length (without bayonet):	94cm	93.5cm	94cm
Length of barrel:	45cm	45cm	45cm
Weight (without mag and bayonet):	3.43kg	3.54kg	4.05kg
Mag capacity:	30 rounds	30 rounds	30 rounds
Effective range:	500m	400m	500m
Rate of fire (cyclic):	630rpm	630rpm	600rpm
Rate of fire (auto):	100rpm	100rpm	100rpm
Rate of fire (single shots):	40rpm	40rpm	40rpm

BERETTA SPECIAL CARBINE SC-70/.223 SHORT VERSION

There are three basic weapons in this Beretta rifle family:

1 AR Assault Rifle with a detachable rigid stock
2 SC Special Carbine with a detachable folding stock
3 LMG with a heavy barrel, carrying handle, bipod and a rigid stock.

Their system of operation is rotating bolt, gas-operated, they fire the 5.56mm × 45mm cartridge with a m/v of 970m/s and fire either full automatic or single shots. They are provided with a grenade launcher (for 40mm Mecar grenades) which also acts as a flash suppressor, the grenade launching sight is a part of the aperture sight assembly. Accessories include a bayonet, telescopic sight sling and bipod.

Beretta Special Carbine and below the short model of the Special Carbine.

Recently Beretta have developed a short version of the Special Carbine, this has been designed for the use of infantry mounted in MICVs and the weapon can be used through firing ports.

The Malaysian Army has purchased large numbers of the Assault Rifle model. The Beretta AR70-78 is a further development of the LMG and features a heavier and detachable barrel.

Further development of the AR70 LMG has resulted in the AR70-78 LMG which has a heavier and detachable barrel.

7.62mm Beretta BM59 Rifle Italy

Data: BM59 Ital
Calibre: 7.62mm
Length: 123.5cm (with bayonet)
109.5cm (without bayonet)
Length of barrel: 49.1cm
Weight: 5.65kg (with loaded mag, bayonet and sling)
4.4kg (without accessories)
Mag capacity: 20 rounds
Range: 600m
Rate of fire: 800rpm (cyclic)
120rpm (auto)
40rpm (single shots)

After the end of World War II Beretta built large numbers of the American M1 Garland Rifle and the BM59 is a development of this but chambered for the 7.62mm × 51mm NATO cartridge. Various models have been developed. The standard rifle of the Italian Army is the BM59 Ital which is fitted with a bipod (this model is sometimes known as the Mk 1), the BM59 Ital Alpini has a pistol grip, folding metal stock and a winter trigger, the BM59 Ital Para is like the Ital Alpini but has a detachable grenade launcher, the BM59 Mk11 is a streamlined version of the basic rifle without the grenade launcher, and without the winter trigger and bipod, the BM59E is a simplified version with a flash hider, cartridge clip guide and 20-round magazine.

The BM59 can fire either single shots or full automatic and can also fire anti-personnel and anti-tank grenades.

Below: The Beretta BM59 Ital.

Centre: The Beretta BM59 Ital Alpini.

Folgore Anti-Tank Weapon Italy

Calibre: 80mm
Length: 150cm
Weight: 10.8kg (launcher only)
Range: 50-75m (min)
500-700m (max)
Crew: 1-2

The Folgore anti-tank weapon has been developed by Breda-Meccanica Bresciana with the assistance of

Snia Viscosa. It is now in its final stages of development but is not yet in production.

The weapon is provided with an optical sight, stabilising leg and a carrying handle. The projectile is fin-stabilised and rocket-assisted, weighs 4.8kg, is 60cm in length, muzzle velocity is 650m/s.

9mm SCK Model 65 Sub-Machine Gun   Japan

Calibre: 9mm
Length: 76.2cm (stock extended)
50.2cm (stock folded)
Weight: 3.35kg
Mag capacity: 30 rounds
Muzzle velocity: 381m/s
Max effective range: 200m
Rate of fire: 550rpm (cyclic)

Produced by the Shin Choo Kogyo KK, Tokyo, the SCK was first manufactured in 1960, and it now equips many Japanese Self Defence Force units. The design has features taken from the American M3A1, the Danish Madsen and the British Sten, and uses a conventional blowback mechanism. The Model 66 is almost identical to the Model 65 but has a slower rate of fire (465rpm).

7.62mm Type 64 Rifle   Japan

Calibre: 7.62mm
Length: 99cm
Length of barrel: 45cm
Weight: 4.3kg (with bipod but without mag)
.487kg (loaded mag)
Mag capacity: 20 rounds
Muzzle velocity: 700m/s (reduced charge)
800m/s (full charge)
Range: 400m
Rate of fire: 470rpm (cyclic)
100rpm (rapid fire)
20rpm (sustained)

The Type 64 is the standard rifle of the Japanese Self Defence Force and was designed and built by the Howa Machinery Company Limited.

The weapon fires a standard 7.62mm × 51mm NATO cartridge but with a reduced charge to suit the stature of the Japanese soldier. The gas regulator can be adjusted to launch rifle grenades or for full charge cartridges. It is gas-operated and the method of locking is of the tilting block type.

The fore sight is of the blade type and the rear sight is of the aperture type and graduated for 200 and 400m. A bipod is provided.

7.62mm Type 62 Machine Gun   Japan

Calibre: 7.62mm
Length: 120cm
Length of barrel: 63.5cm
Weight: 10.7kg
Muzzle velocity: 855m/s
Range: 600m (bipod)
1,100m (tripod)

The Type 62 Machine Gun was designed by the Nittoku Metal Industry Company and is the standard machine gun of the Japanese Self Defence Force. It entered service in 1962.

The weapon is gas-operated and fires the NATO 7.62mm × 51mm cartridge and is fed from a disintegrating link belt. It is air-cooled, full automatic and has a quick change barrel. The fore sight is of the blade type and the rear sight is of the leaf apperture type. A bipod is provided and the weapon can be

mounted on a tripod for the sustained fire role if required and in this role the bipod is folded up underneath the barrel. A telescopic sight is also available.

The latest Japanese machine gun is the 7.62mm Type 74 which can be mounted on a tripod for use in the ground role as well as being used as an anti-aircraft gun on AFVs (including the STB MBT). The Type 74 is 108.5cm long and has a barrel length of 62.5cm, muzzle velocity is 750m/s.

7.65mm Type 64 Pistol

Korea (North)

Calibre: 7.65mm
Length: 17.1cm
Length of barrel: 10.2cm
Weight: .624kg
Mag capacity: 7 rounds
Muzzle velocity: 290m/s
Effective range: 30m

The 7.65mm Type 64 pistol is a North Korean copy of the Browning Model 1900 pistol and has the stamping '1964 7.62' on the left side although it is chambered for the 7.65mm × 17mm SR cartridge. A silenced version is known as the Type 64 as well, this has a shortened slide to allow for the attachment of the screw on silencer. The North Korean Type 68 pistol is based on the Russian M-1933 (TT-33) pistol but is both shorter and bulkier as well as being mechanically different.

9mm Model HM-3 Sub-Machine Gun

Mexico

Calibre: 9mm
Length: 63.5cm
Length of barrel: 25.5cm
Weight: 2.69kg (without mag)
3.345kg (with loaded mag)
Mag capacity: 32 rounds

This 9mm sub-machine gun is manufactured by Productos Mendoza SA and fires a standard 9mm × 19mm Parabellum cartridge. Its method of operation is blowback and the user can select either full automatic or single shots. The original model had a fixed wire type stock but the latest model (called the Improved HM-3) has a folding stock which folds forwards through 180° and then acts as a forestock. The improved model weighs 2.98kg empty.

9mm P-64 Pistol

Poland

Calibre: 9mm
Length: 15.5cm
Length of barrel: 8.46cm
Weight: .68kg (loaded)
.636kg (empty)
Mag capacity: 6 rounds
Muzzle velocity: 305m/s
Max effective range: 50m

The P-64 pistol has replaced the Soviet Pistolet TT in Polish Army service. It is conventional in design and has used some of the features of the Walther PP. It fires a 9mm × 18mm cartridge. The P-64 uses a double action trigger and the safety catch is on the left. The weapon is issued complete with a holster, spare magazine and a cleaning rod.

9mm PM-63 Machine Pistol

Poland

Calibre: 9mm
Length: 58.3cm (stock extended)
33.3cm (stock folded)
Length of barrel: 15cm
Weight: 1.8kg (loaded, 25 rounds)
1.55kg (empty)
Mag capacity: 15, 25 and 40 rounds
Muzzle velocity: 320m/s
Max effective range: 200m (stock extended)
40m (without stock)
Rate of fire: 650rpm (cyclic)
75rpm (auto)
40rpm (single shots)

The Pistolet Maszynowy PM-63 is also known as the Mini-Pistol and is similar in concept to the Czech

Skorpion machine pistol. The PM-63 fires the 9mm × 18mm Markarov round and is blowback operated. It is unusual in having no fire-selector as such as full or semi-automatic fire is achieved by trigger pressure. For accurate fire on full automatic a folding metal stock is fitted. A good recognition feature is the trough-like compensator above the muzzle which is supposed to keep the muzzle down on automatic fire. The PM-63 is issued with a sling, hip holster, cleaning rod and four magazines. To date the PM-63 appears to have been used by paratroop and crews of AFVs only.

9mm FBP M 48 Sub-Machine Gun Portugal

Calibre: 9mm
Length: 81.3cm (stock extended)
63.5cm (stock retracted)
Length of barrel: 24.9cm
Weight: 4.43kg (loaded)
Mag capacity: 32 rounds
Muzzle velocity: 381m/s
Max effective range: 200m
Rate of fire: 500rpm (cyclic)

This Portuguese design is a combination of a German MP40 bolt (with some changes) in a receiver based on that of the American M3 SMG. The M48 is in service with the Portuguese Army and may therefore also be encountered in the parts of Africa where the Portuguese have been involved.

9mm M1941 (Orita) Sub-Machine Gun Romania

Calibre: 9mm
Length: 89.4cm
Length of barrel: 28.7cm
Weight: 4kg (loaded)
3.45kg (empty)
Mag capacity: 25 or 32 rounds
Muzzle velocity: 381m/s
Max effective range: 200m
Rate of fire: 400rpm (cyclic)
120rpm (auto)
50rpm (semi-auto)

The Orita was built at the Cugir Arsenal in Romania from 1941 to 1944. Although it is no longer in front-line service, it is still used by the Workers' Militia. There are two models — one has a folding metal stock rather like that used on the German MP40 and the other uses a conventional wooden stock. Construction is robust as all parts were machined from solid, a factor which no doubt explains the weapon's longevity. Operation is simple blowback, and one unusual feature is that the rear sight is calibrated up to 500m.

9mm Makarov (PM) Pistol Soviet Union

Calibre: 9mm
Length: 16cm
Length of barrel: 9.3cm
Weight: .81kg (with loaded mag)
.73kg (with empty mag)
.675kg (without mag)
Mag capacity: 8 rounds
Range: 50m

The 9mm Makarov pistol was introduced into the Soviet Army after World War II and is very similar in appearance to the Walther PP pistol. The Makarov is an eight-shot, blowback, magazine-fed pistol with a double-action trigger. This allows the hammer, if uncocked, to be cocked and released by a single long

pull on the trigger. The weapon is also manufactured in East Germany and Communist China. The East German model is known as the Pistole M and has no lanyard loop and plain grips, the Soviet model has a star on its grips. The Communist Chinese model is known as the Type 59 and has the markings 59 SHI on the receiver. The Makarov has a double action trigger and its rate of fire is 30 rounds per minute. It fires the 9mm × 18mm cartridge, these have a m/v of 315m/s. The front sight is of the blade type and the rear sight is of the V-notch type.

The 9mm Makarov (PM) pistol.

9mm Stechkin (APS) Pistol

Soviet Union

Calibre: 9mm
Length: 54cm (with stock)
Length of pistol: 22.5cm
Length of barrel: 18.5cm
Weight: 1.78kg (with loaded mag and holster)
1.22kg (with loaded mag)
1.02kg (with empty mag)
Magazine capacity: 20 rounds
Range: 50m (practical)
150/220m (max with stock)

The 9mm Stechkin (APS) pistol was introduced after World War II and is now in very limited use. This weapon is a machine pistol as it has both semi-automatic (40rpm) or full automatic (90rpm) capability. The selector is on the left side of the receiver and has three positions — safe, semi-automatic and full automatic. To enable the weapon to be fired more accurately at longer ranges the wooden holster can be attached to the grip. The front sight is of the blade type and the rear-sight is a V notch that can be adjusted for 25, 50, 100 and 200m ranges. The weapon fires the same 9mm round with a m/v of 340m/s as the Makarov pistol. When being carried in the holster the grips of the Strechkin protrude.

The 9mm Strechkin (APS) pistol.

7.62mm Tula Tokarev M-1933 (or TT-33) Pistol

Soviet Union

Calibre: 7.62mm
Length: 19.5cm
Length of barrel: 11.6cm
Weight: .94.kg (with loaded mag)
.854kg (with empty mag)
.769kg (without mag)
Mag capacity: 8 rounds
Range: 45-50m

The TT-33 is based on a modified Colt-Browning design and has been replaced in the Soviet Army by the 9mm Marakov pistol. The TT-33 has been made in many countries including the following:
Soviet Union: With letters CCCP on the grips.
Poland: With letters FB on the grips.
Hungary: This is known as the 48M and has also been made, in 9mm calibre. This model is known as the Tokagypt 58.
Communist China: Two models — the Type 51 and Type 54.
Yugoslavia: Known as the M-57. The M70(d) is the M-57 chambered to fire the 9mm Parabelleum round.
North Korea: Known as Type 68 and based on TT-33.
In most cases the foreign weapons differ in small details to the original Soviet weapon.

The TT-33 fires the 7.62mm × 25mm Type P round which has a muzzle velocity of 420m/s. The weapon has no safety catch — the hammer is set at the half-cock position. The front sight is of the blade type and the rear is of the U-notch type.

7.62mm Sudayev M1943 (PPS) Sub-Machine Gun

Soviet Union

Calibre: 7.62mm
Length: 83.1cm (stock extended)
61.6cm (stock folded)
Length of barrel: 27cm
Weight: 3.62kg (with loaded box mag)
3.24kg (with empty box mag)
3kg (without mag)
Mag capacity: 35 rounds
Range: 200m (short bursts)
100m (long bursts)

The M1943(PPS) SMG was developed from the earlier PPS M1942 SMG during the early part of World War II. The weapon is no longer in front-line service with any of the Warsaw Pact Forces. It can only be operated as a full automatic although it is said that an experienced soldier can fire single rounds by touching the trigger in a certain way!

The PPS M1943 is of all-metal construction except for the grips which are of plastic. The metal shoulder stock can be folded along the top of the receiver when not required. The ejection port is on the right side of the receiver. The M1943 fires the 7.62mm × 25mm cartridge which has a m/v of 500m/s, cyclic rate of fire is 650rpm, practical rate of fire is 100rpm. The front sight is of the post type and the rear sight is of the L-type with a notch.

After World War II the Polish Army produced a model of this weapon with a number of modifications including a wooden stock and this was known as the M43/52. It has also been manufactured in Communist China as the Type 43 SMG.

7.62mm Shpagin M1941 (PPSh) Sub-Machine Gun Soviet Union

Calibre: 7.62mm
Length: 84.2cm
Length of barrel: 27cm
Weight: 5.3kg (with loaded drum mag)
4.1kg (with loaded box mag)
4.6kg (with empty drum mag)
3.78kg (with empty box mag)
3.5kg (without mag)
Mag capacity: 71-round drum
35-round box
Range: 200m (short bursts)
100m (long bursts)

This weapon was developed during World War II and is no longer in front line use with the Soviet Army although it is still used in many other parts of the world, especially the Middle and Far East.

It can be used either as a semi-automatic or as a full automatic and the change lever is on the trigger guard, forward for automatic and rearward for semi-automatic. It fires the M1930 'P' 7.62mm × 25mm round, m/v being 500m/s, cyclic rate of fire is 700/900rpm but for practical purposes its rate of fire on semi-automatic is 40/50rpm and on full automatic 90/100rpm. Early weapons had the drum type magazine but later models normally had the

curved box magazine. The front sights are of the hooded post type with the rear sights either tangent leaf (early models) or flip notch (later models).

The Shpagin M1941 (PPSh) has also been built in many other countries including:
Communist China: Built as the Type 50 SMG, has box type magazine only, rear sight has apertures.
Hungary: Built as the Type 48M, V-notch rear sight.
Iran: Built both in 7.62mm and 9mm calibres, V-notch rear sight.
North Korea: Built as the Type 49 with aperture rear sight.
North Vietnam: Built as the Type K-50M, this is a Type 50 with a retractable metal stock (qv).
Yugoslavia: Built with many modifications as the M-49 or M-49/59 (qv).

7.62mm Modernised Kalashnikov (AKM) Assault Rifle

Soviet Union

	AKM	AKMS
Calibre:	7.62cm	7.62cm
Length:	102cm	102cm (with bayonet)
	88cm	88cm (rifle only)
	——	64cm (stock folded)
Length of barrel:	41.5cm	41.5cm
Weight:	3.6kg	3.8kg (loaded aluminium mag)
	3.76kg	3.96kg (loaded late steel mag)
	3.86kg	4.06kg (loaded early steel mag)
	3.1kg	3.3kg (empty aluminium mag)
	3.26kg	3.46kg (empty late steel mag)
	3.36kg	3.56kg (empty early steel mag)
	2.93kg	3.13kg (without mag)
Mag capacity:	30 rounds	30 rounds
Range:	400m	400m (semi-auto)
	300m	300m (auto)
Rate of fire:	600rpm	600rpm (cyclic)
	100rpm	100rpm (auto practical)
	40rpm	40rpm (semi-auto practical)

The AKM is a development of the AK-47 assault rifle and the most significant difference is in the construction of the receiver. Ther AK-47 has a forged and machined receiver whilst the AKM has a stamped receiver. Mechanically, the weapons are very similar but the AKM has a cyclic rate reducer in its trigger mechanism. As with the AK-47 there are two models of the AKM. The basic model which has a wooden stock is known as the AKM whilst that with a folding stock is known as the AKMS. Recognition features include radial gas ports on the gas cylinder, grasping rails on the handguard and the bayonet-lug. The fore sight is of the pillar type with the rear sight of the V-notch type and graduated from 200 to 1,000m (the AK-47 is graduated to 800m). It can also be fitted with the NSP-2 infra red night sight. The AKM fires the same 7.62mm × 39mm cartridge with a m/v of 717m/s. The weapon has the same accessories as the AK-47 but its bayonet is of a different design and can also be used as a wire-cutter.

The AKM has also been built in a number of other countries including besides Poland:

East Germany: (MPiKM) One is a standard model with a conventional stock but with plastic grips and plastic handguard. The secod model has a plastic stock, plastic grips and plastic handguard. The folding stock is known as the MPiKMS) They also have cleaning rods. In addition there is a training model which fires a .22 cartridge and is known as the KKMPi-1.

Hungary: Hungarian-built AKMs have a perforated sheet metal forearm with a nylon foregrip. An SMG model has also been built with a muzzle-brake, rear sight graduated to 800m only and a folding stock.

Romania: AKMs have a wooden pistol grip integral with the forestock.

The AKM entered service in 1959 and is both lighter than the AK-47 and easier to manufacture. More recently plastic and aluminium have been introduced into the weapon.

The East German MPiKM assault rifle with a plastic stock.

10

Above: The 7.62mm AKMS assault rifle with a folding stock.

Below: Romanian AKM with wooden pistol grip integral with forestock.

7.62mm Kalashnikov (AK-47) Assault Rifle   Soviet Union

	Early Model	Late Model
Calibre:	7.62mm	7.62mm
Length:	107cm	107cm (with bayonet)
	87cm	87cm (stock extended)
	64.5cm	64.5cm (stock folded)
Length of barrel:	41.5cm	41.5cm
Weight:	4.53kg	4.14kg (loaded aluminium mag)
	4.69kg	4.3kg (loaded late steel mag)
	4.79kg	4.4kg (loaded early steel mag)
	4.04kg	3.64kg (empty aluminium mag)
	4.2kg	3.8kg (empty late steel mag)
	4.3kg	3.9kg (empty early steel mag)
	3.87kg	3.47kg (without mag)
Mag capacity:	30 rounds	30 rounds
Range:	400m	400m (semi-auto)
	300m	300m (auto)
Rate of fire:	600rpm	600rpm (cyclic)
	100rpm	100rpm (auto practical)
	40rpm	40rpm (semi-auto)

The AK-47 was designed shortly after the end of World War II by Mikhail Kalashnikov and entered service with the Russian Army in 1951. It is no longer in front line service with the Warsaw Pact Forces having been replaced by the AKM which was developed from the AK-47.

The AK-47 has been built with both a wooden stock and a folding metal stock and there are also differences between early and late production models. Early models had a built-up receiver while late models had a straight rear ends to their receivers.

The AK-47 is gas-operated and fires a 7.62mm × 39mm cartridge with a m/v of 717m/s. It is capable of full or semi-automatic fire, the selector is on the RHS of the receiver (up for safe, centre for automatic and down for semi-automatic). Its sights are graduated to 800m. The fore sight is of the pillar type and the rear sight is of the U-notch type.

The accessories for the AK-47 comprise a combination tool kit, a bayonet (two types — not interchangeable with those of the AKM, sling, blank firing device, night operations equipment (NSP-2 infra-red sight and a luminous sight), and a magazine carrier. There are four types of magazine for this weapon, two steel, one aluminium and one plastic.

The AK-47 has been manufactured in a number of countries including:
Bulgaria
Communist China: Known as the Type 56 assault rifle and similar to the later production Russian models; recent models have a folding spike type bayonet. Type 56-1 is similar to the Soviet folding stock model.
Czechoslovakia: Although similar in appearance the *Czech* Vzor 58 assault rifle is in fact a different weapon in design.

Top: The standard 7.62mm Kalashnikov AK-47 assault rifle with wooden stock.

Above: The 7.62mm AK-47 with a folding metal stock.

East Germany: Known as the MPiK and MPiKS (folding butt). These do not have cleaning rods under the barrel or a recess in the butt for cleaning tools.
Finland: See M60 and M62 assault rifles .
Hungary
North Korea: Known as the Type 58 Assault Rifle.
Poland: The basic AK-47 is known as the PMK. The PMK-DGN-60 is used for launching the following grenades — DGN-60 HEAT anti-tank grenade with a range of 100m and the F1/N60 Fragmentation grenade with a range of 100/240m; this weapon has a 10-round magazine.
Romania
Yugoslavia: three models, see separate entry (page 129.

7.62mm Dragunov (SVD) Sniper's Rifle   Soviet Union

Calibre: 7.62mm
Length: 122.5cm
137cm (with bayonet)
Length of barrel: 62cm
Weight: 4.78kg (with 'scope, loaded mag and bayonet)
4.52kg (with 'scope and loaded mag)

4.3kg (with 'scope and empty mag)
3.72kg (without 'scope and with empty mag)
3.51kg (without 'scope and mag)
Mag capacity: 10 rounds
Range: 1,300m (with 'scope)
800m (without 'scope)

The 7.62mm Dragunov SVD sniper's rifle has replaced the M1891/30 sniper's rifle in the Warsaw Pact Forces. The weapon is easily recognisable by its skeleton stock with its small cheekpad, curved magazine and its sporting type barrel with gas cylinder above the barrel. A flash-suppressor is fitted at the end of the barrel and a standard AKM bayonet can be fitted if required. It fires the 7.62mm × 54mm R round with a m/v of 830m/s and its maximum rate of fire is 30rpm. The Dragunov is a gas-operated semi-automatic weapon and is related to the AK-47 family of weapons. Its normal sights are graduated to 1,200m. The PSO-1 telescopic sight has a ×4 magnification and a 6° field of view. It also has an integral rangefinder, a battery-powered reticle illumination system and an infra-red reconnaissance aid. This weighs 58kg and is graduated to 1,300m.

Dragunov (SVD) Sniper's Rifle.

7.62mm Simonov (SKS) Carbine   Soviet Union

Calibre: 7.62mm
Length: 126cm (bayonet extended)
102cm (bayonet folded)
Length of barrel: 52cm
Weight: 4.01kg (loaded mag)
3.85kg (empty mag)
Mag capacity: 10 rounds
Effective range: 400m

The Simonov carbine was designed by S. G. Simonov in 1944 and was standardised in 1945 as the 7.62mm semi-automatic carbine Simonov (SKS). It is no longer in front-line use with the Soviet Army having been replaced by the Kalashnikov assault rifle. It is, however, still used for ceremonial purposes.

Early production models had a needle type folding bayonet but this was soon replaced by a knife type bayonet. The SKS is gas-operated and semi-automatic, it fires the 7.62mm × 39mm cartridge, m/v being 735m/s. Normal rate of fire is 30rpm.

It is provided with a hooded front post and a rear tangent sight, and is sighted to 1,000m at 100m intervals. The SKS is easily recognisable by its bayonet, triangular integral magazine forward of the trigger and the gas port cylinder above the barrel. The Simonov has also been built in the following countries:
Communist China: known as the Type 56 with folding needle bayonet.
East Germany: known as the Karbiner S, also has a slot in the stock for attaching end of sling.
North Korea: built and known as the Type 63.
Yugoslavia: early models known as the M-59, later modified models were known as the M-59/66 (qv).
As far as is known there are none of the following rifles left in service with the Soviet or any other army: Self-Loading 7.62mm Tokarev (SVT.38) Rifle, Self-Loading 7.62mm Tokarev (SVT 1940) Rifle, 7.62mm Tokarev Automatic Rifle (AVT 1940) and the 7.62mm Simonov Automatic Rifle (AVS 36).

7.62mm Moisin Nagant M1944 Carbine   Soviet Union

Calibre: 7.62mm
Length: 133cm (with bayonet)
101.6cm (carbine only)
Length of barrel: 51.8cm
Weight: 4.02kg (loaded with bayonet)
3.9kg (empty with bayonet)
Mag capacity: 5 rounds
Range: 400m

This is the carbine version of the M1891/30 rifle and is recognisable by its permanently attached needle bayonet which folds along the RHS when not in use. The earlier M1938 carbine is very similar but does not have a folding bayonet.

The M1944 fires the 7.62mm × 54mmR round the m/v is 820m/s and average rate of fire is 10rpm Its front sight is of the hooded post type and its rea sight is of the tangent notch type.

This weapon is no longer in front-line use with an of the Warsaw Pact Countries. It has been built i Communist China under the designation Type 5. Carbine. The Vietnamese used the Type 53 or th M1944 fitted with a spigot type grenade launche known as the AT-44 rifle.

The 7.62mm Moisin Nagant M1944 carbine.

7.62mm Moisin Nagant M1891/30 Rifle   Soviet Union

Calibre: 7.62mm
Length: 123cm
Length of barrel: .83m
Weight: 5.1kg (excluding sling)
Mag capacity: 5 rounds
Max effective range: 800m

This rifle entered service in 1930 and continued in production until 1944 and was one of the standard rifles of the Soviet Army during World War II. It was replaced by the M-1944.

The Moisin Nagant M1891/30 has a hooded post front sight, the rear sight is an adjustable tangent leaf sight with a V-notch. Usual rate of fire is 10rpm and it has a m/v of 862m/s. This weapon is also used as a sniper's rifle although this has been replaced in the Soviet Army by the new SVD rifle. The basic rifle has a straight bolt handle and the sniper's model has

a longer turned-down handle. The sniper's model car be fitted with various types of telescope includin the PE with a range of 1,400m and the PU with range of 1,300m. The sniper's model does not hav a bayonet. Both of these rifles fire the 7.62mm × 54mmR rimmed round. The M1891/30 can b recognised by its sling holes in the stock, shor straight bolt handle and its protruding magazine.

Other similar models to the M1891/30 rifle ar the M1910 (no bayonet) and M1938 carbines an the M1891 (Dragon) rifle. The M1944 carbine is shortened model of the M1891/30 and has permanently attached folding needle type bayonet.

The 7.62mm Moisin Nagant M1891/30 rifle.

7.62mm Kalashnikov (RPK)
Light Machine Gun

The 7.62mm Kalashnikov LMG (RPK) Romanian model.

Calibre: 7.62mm
Length: 103.5cm (overall)
82cm (RPKS with folded stock)
Length of barrel: 59.1cm
Weight: 7.1kg (loaded drum)
5.9kg (loaded box)
5.9kg (empty drum)
5.3kg (empty box)
5kg (without mag)
Mag capacity: 30-round AK-47/AKM box mag
40-round RPK box mag
75-round RPK drum mag
Range: 800m
Rate of fire: 600rpm (cyclic)
50/150rpm (practical)

The RPK is a gas-operated, selective-fire weapon that has been developed from the AK-47 assault rifle and is the replacement for the RPD LMG.

The main differences between the AK-47 and the RPK are that the latter has a longer and heavier barrel, folding bipod, modified receiver, different rear sight and a different forearm and shoulder stock. The basic weapon is the RPK, the RPKS has a folding stock and this is normally issued to airborne troops.

The weapon fires the 7.62mm × 39mm M1943 cartridge with a m/v of 732m/s and uses the same accessories as the AK-47 with the exception of the bayonet. Like the AK-47 the AKM can be fitted with an infra-red night sight. The RPK selector has three positions safe (top), full automatic (centre) and single shot (bottom). Its fore sight is of the cylindrical post type and its rear sight is of the leaf notch type sighted from 100 to 1,000m. The East Germans call the RPK the 1MG-K. North Vietnam produces a similar weapon called the TUL-1. This is based on the Chinese Type 56 (AK-47) assault rifle and is fed from a 75-round drum.

7.62mm Degtyarev (RPD)
Light Machine Gun

Calibre: 7.62mm
Length: 103.7cm
Length of barrel: 52.3cm
Weight: 9kg (loaded drum)
7.4kg (empty drum)
6.6kg (without mag)
Mag capacity: 100 rounds
Range: 800m
Rate of fire: 650rpm (cyclic)
150rpm (practical)

The RPD (Ruchnoi Pulemet Degtyarev) entered production shortly after the end of World War II as a replacement for the DP and DPM LMGs. The RPD has itself now been replaced by the RPK LMG.

The RPD is recognisable by its short wooden stock, bipod, pistol-grip behind the trigger-guard and a wooden hand-grip forward of the drum magazine. The RPD is a gas-operated full automatic weapon and fires the 7.62mm × 39mm cartridge with a m/v of 753m/s. The drum holds two 50-round belts. The fore sight is of the cylindrical post type and the rear sight is of the leaf tangent type sighted from 100 to 1,000m in increments of 100m. The NSP-2 night sighting devices can be used with this weapon.

There have been many models of the RPD LMG. These include the 1st model which had a cup type gas piston; the 2nd model which had a plunger type gas piston in place of the cup type and the windage knob was moved from the RS to the LS; the 3rd model was similar to the 2nd model but had dust covers on the feed mechanism and a folding non-reciprocating operating handle. This model was also built in Communist China as the Type 56; the 4th model is also known as the RPDM and is similar to the 3rd model but has a longer gas cylinder, an additional roller on the piston slide and a buffer in the butt; the 5th model was built only in Communist China where it was known as the Type 56-1, and is essentially a model RPDM with a magazine bracket/dust cover and a cleaning rod which is carried in the butt.

The RPD was built in a number of other countries including Hungary and North Korea, the Korean weapons being known as the Type 62.

7.62mm Kalashnikov (PK, PKS, PKT) General Purpose Machine Gun Soviet Union

Calibre: 7.62mm
Length: 117.3cm
Length of barrel: 65.8cm (with flash suppressor)
Weight: 16.5kg (on tripod)
9kg (on bipod)
9.4kg (ammo box and 250-round belt)
8kg (ammo box and 200-round belt)
3.9kg (ammo box and 100-round belt)
Range: 1,000m
Rate of fire: 650rpm (cyclic)
250rpm (practical)

This is the current GPMG of most of the Warsaw Pact Forces and was designed by Kalashnikov who also designed the AK-47 assault rifle. The bolt mechanism is similar to that of the AK-47, the feed mechanism is similar to that of the Goryunov and Czech M59 weapons whilst the trigger mechanism is similar to that used on the Degtyarev MG.

When used with its bipod it is an LMG; ammunition is fed from a 100-round box magazine attached to the weapon. When used on a tripod (it still retains

the bipod which folds up under the barrel when not required) it is fed from a 200- or 250-round box which is placed on the ground to the right of the weapon, which is then used as a heavy machine gun. When fitted in an AFV it is used as a coaxial weapon and operated by an electric trigger. It is then known as the PKT. The PKB is used externally on armoured vehicles.

A more recent model is the PKM — this is somewhat lighter than the earlier models. The barrel is unfluted and it also has a number of other modifications including a hinged butt rest. The PKMS is the PKM on a tripod.

The PK is belt-fed, air-cooled, and fully automatic. It fires the 7.62mm × 54mmR cartridge with a m/v of 825m/s. Its gas regulator can be adjusted if required. The weapon is recognisable by its gas cylinder below the barrel, its frame type stock, carrying handle, pistol grip and folding bipod.

7.62mm PK machine gun.

The barrel on the PK can be changed quickly. Early models had a cone shaped flash-hider but more recent models have a bar type supressor fitted similar to that on the American M60 MG. The PK has a cylindrical fore sight and an adjustable rear sight. If required it can be fitted with an infra-red night fighting device.

7.62mm PKT machine gun as installed in AFVs.

It replaced the earlier RP-46 and SGM machine guns.

7.62mm RP-46 Machine Gun Soviet Union

Calibre: 7.62mm
Length: 127cm
Length of barrel: 60cm
Weight: 15.8kg (loaded drum)
14.57kg (empty drum)
13kg (without drum or belt)
9.63kg (ammo box and 250-round belt)
Mag capacity: 250-round belt
47-round drum
Range: 800-1,000m
Rate of fire: 230/250rpm (practical)
600rpm (cyclic)
Crew: 2

The 7.62mm RP-46 machine gun. (Type 58 shown.)

The RP-46 MG is a postwar development of the DPM range. It is no longer in service with the Soviet forces but is still used by China, North Korea, Vietnam and various 'Liberation Armies'. It has a carrying handle above the barrel rather like the British Bren LMG, a quick change barrel, bipod,

pistol-grip, and an operating-spring housing which projects at the rear of the receiver. It fires the 7.62mm × 54mmR cartridge with a m/v of 840m/s. Although it can use a 47-round drum magazine (as used on the DP and DPM LMGs but without the belt feed mechanism), it normally uses a box with 250 rounds in 50-round metallic link belts. The PPN-2 night sighting device can be fitted to the RP-46. This weapon is also manufactured in Communist China as the Type 58 and in North Korea as the Type 64.

89

7.62mm Goryunov M-1943 (SG-43) Machine Gun

Calibre: 7.62mm
Length: 115cm
Length of barrel: 82.5cm (with flash hider)
72cm (without flash hider)
Weight: 36.9kg (gun and new wheeled mount)
40.4kg (gun and old wheeled mount)
27.4kg (gun and tripod)
13.5kg (gun only)
9.08kg (ammo box and 250-round belt)
Mag capacity: 250-round fabric belt
50-round metallic belt
Range: 800/1,000m
500m anti-aircraft
Rate of fire: 250/300rpm (practical)
500/700prm (cyclic)
Crew: 2

The 7.62mm Goryunov MG entered service with the Russian Army during World War II and is no longer in front line service with the Soviet forces. The first model to enter service was the SG; this had a smooth barrel, the sear attached to the driving-spring guide, a plain barrel lock, no dust covers and

the operating handle between the spade grips. The second model was the SGM which has a splined barrel, a separate sear housing, a micrometer barrel lock and the operating handle on the right side of the weapon. The SGMT was a modified version for use on tanks and the SGMB was a modified version for use on armoured personnel carriers. The SG-43M is a reworked SG with the dust covers and barrel lock as with the SGMB. The last model is a GPMG type weapon developed by the Hungarians complete with pistol-grip trigger mechanism, butt stock and a bipod.

There are three types of mount for this weapon. The first M-1943 mount was on two wheels as was the latter Degtyarev mount. The more recent mount is the Sidorenko-Malinovsky tripod.

The weapon fires the 7.62mm × 54mmR round which has a m/v of 800m/s. Its front sight is of the blade type and its rear sight consists of an adjustable tangent leaf graduated from 200 to 2,300m in increments of 100m.

The SG is built in Communist China as the Type 53 whilst the SGMB is built there as the Type 57.

7.62mm Degtyarev DP and DPM Light Machine Guns

Data: DPM
Calibre: 7.62mm
Length: 127cm
Length of barrel: 60.9cm
Weight: 11.9kg (loaded drum)
10.7kg (empty drum)
9.1kg (without drum)
Mag capacity: 47-round drum
Range: 600m (practical)
Rate of fire: 550rpm (cyclic)
80rpm (practical)

The DP LMG was developed in the 1920s by Degtyarev and entered production in 1933. It was the standard LMG of the Soviet Army during World War II. The DP is gas-operated and full automatic firing the 7.62mm × 54mmR round which has a m/v of 840m/s. The DA was an aircraft machine gun and the DT was a tank machine gun which had a folding stock and no barrel jacket.

The DPM, the M standing for modernised, was introduced in 1944. The modifications over the earlier DP included the fitting of a pistol-grip and a permanent bipod and the operating spring was removed from its position under the barrel, it is now longer and projects over the butt. The DPM has been built in Communist China as the Type 53 LMG. The DPM was subsequently modified further to become the RP-46 (qv). Neither of these weapons are now in front line Soviet use.

Photograph shows the Type 53 LMG, the Chinese version of the DPM.

7.62mm Maxim M1910 (SPM) Machine Gun

Soviet Union

Calibre: 7.62mm
Length: 111cm
Length of barrel: 72cm
Weight: 69kg (gun, mount and shield)
46.38kg (gun, old type mount and no shield)
23.8kg (gun and coolant)
21.4kg (gun only)
9.08kg (ammo box and a 250-round belt of ammo)
Range: 1,000m (ground role)
500m (anti-aircraft role)
Rate of fire: 250/300rpm (practical)
500/600rpm (cyclic)
Crew: 2-3

The Maxim M1910 MG was adopted by the Russian Army before the start of World War I and continued in service with them until soon after the end of World War II. The first Maxims originated in England but in 1905 the Russians set up their own production line. The first model produced was the M1905 which had a bronze water-jacket, this was followed by the M1910 which had a plain steel water-jacket, the next model had a fluted casing and the final model (from 1942) had a large radiator type filler-cap on the top of the jacket. There were two mounts for the Maxim. The usual World War II mount was the so-called Sokolov mount, which often had a shield, the second was the universal mount which could also be used in the anti-aircraft role.

The 7.62mm Maxim M1910 fires the 7.62mm × 54mmR cartridge, m/v 800m/s. Its front sight is of the protected blade type and the rear sight is of the adjustable folding V-notch type.

The Maxim was phased out of the WPF many years ago but is still encountered in various parts of the world.

The 7.62mm Maxim M1910 (SPM) machine gun.

12.7mm Degtyarev Shpagin M1938 and M1938/46 DShK Heavy Machine Guns

Calibre: 12.7mm
Length: 158.8cm
Length of barrel: 106.9cm (with flash eliminator)
Weight: 131.5kg (gun and tripod)
34kg (gun only)
11kg (ammo box and 50 rounds)
Mag capacity: 50-round belt
Range: 7,000m (max)
1,500m (effective)
1,000m (anti-aircraft — effective)
Rate of fire: 540/600rpm (cyclic)
80/120rpm (practical)

The DShK entered service with the Soviet Army in 1938 and was a development of the earlier DK machine gun. The weapon is gas-operated and fully automatic, air-cooled and belt-fed. It fires the 12.7mm × 108mm cartridge with a m/v of 860m/s which is fed in belts of 50. There is also an AP round which will penetrate 20mm of armour at 500m. The front sight is of the cylindrical post type and the rear sight is of the vertical leaf type which is graduated from 0-3,300m in increments of 100m. There is also a special AA sight.

The DShK is now used in the Soviet Army as a tank machine gun (ie anti-aircraft with a reflex sight) or as a coaxial machine gun (ie on the T-10 tank). This is known as the DShKT. The DShK is still used in many countries in its original role as an HMG.

The M1938 has a revolving block type feed mechanism with an arched feed cover. The M1938/46 (which is also known as the DShKM) was developed after World War II and has a belt-fed lever type feed mechanism and a rectangular cover. A flash eliminator was also introduced on this model.

The DShK can be used for both ground or anti-aircraft use. For the ground role the three legs are folded together to form the trail and the shield and wheels are retained. In the anti-aircraft role the wheels and the shield are removed and the trail legs form a tripod.

The M1938/46 is also built in China where it is known as the Type 54 HMG. The Czechs have developed a four-gun anti-aircraft model of this called the MG53 which is mounted on a chassis to give increased mobility.

The recognition features of the DShK are its fluted barrel, flash eliminators, its fore sight about a quarter of the way down the barrel, its shield and its firing grips at the rear.

RPG-7V Anti-Tank Grenade Launcher　　　Soviet Union

Calibre: 85mm (launcher)
40mm (tube)
Weight of launcher: 6.3kg (including telescopic sight)
Length of tube: 95cm
Range: 500m (stationary target)
300m (moving target)
Rate of fire: 4-6rpm
Crew: 2

The RPG-7V is the standard rifle-squad anti-tank weapon of the Warsaw Pact Forces and is a recoil-less, shoulder-fired, muzzle-loaded, reloadable weapon. It fires a PG-7V HEAT rocket, 92.5cm in length and weighing 2.2kg, with a muzzle velocity as it leaves the barrel of 100m/s. Within 10m a rocket motor fires and this boosts its velocity to 300m/s. The warhead weighs 1.75kg and will penetrate 32cm of armour. It has a piezo-electric fuse incorporating a self-destruct device which operates when the round is approx 900m from the launcher. There is also a training round called the PUS-7.

This weapon is recognisable by its two handgrips with the trigger on the foremost grip, optical sight on the LHS of the weapon and the funnel-shaped venturi at the rear.

The RPG-7V is fitted with a PGO-7 or PGO-7V optical sight which is marked from 200m to 500m at ranges of 100m. The sight has a ×2.5 magnification and a 13° field of view. Open sights are provided for emergency use. If required this weapon can be fitted with the NSP-2 infra-red night sighting device.

The RPG-7D is a special model for the use of the airborne forces and can be quickly broken down into two components.

The RPG-7V is built in China under the designation of the Type 69 Anti-Tank Grenade Launcher.

The RPG-7V anti-tank grenade launcher.

82mm SPG-82 Anti-Tank Rocket Launcher　　Soviet Union

Calibre: 82mm
Length: 215cm (overall)
206cm (tube)
Weight: 37.85kg (launcher)
Range: 275m (stationary target)
Crew: 2

The SPG-82 is also known as the SG-82 and is easily recognisable by its large shield, two-wheeled carriage and carrying handles. The weapon is no longer in use with any of the Warsaw Pact Forces but is still found in various parts of the world including the Middle East.

The SPG-82 can be fired from the prone position or from the shoulder, in the latter case it has to be supported by two men.

Without its fuse the HEAT projectile is 69.4cm in length and weighs 4.95kg. It has a muzzle velocity of 150m/s and will penetrate 12cm of armour. An HE round is also available for this weapon.

The weapon has two sets of sights. The inner set which is used for the HEAT projectile is marked for 100, 200 and 300m and the outer set, used for the HE round, is marked from 100 to 700m in 100m bands.

RPG-2 Anti-Tank Launcher　　　Soviet Union

Calibre: 80mm (launcher)
40mm (tube)
Length: 95cm (tube)
Weight: 2.86kg (launcher)
Range: 150m (stationary target)
75m (moving target)
Rate of fire: 4-6rpm
Crew: 1 or 2

The first Soviet anti-tank launcher was the RPG-1 which was a direct copy of the German Panzerfaust. The RPG-2 was a development of the German

Panzerfaust 150 which was developed at the end of World War II but did not see service. The RPG-2 is no longer in service with the Soviet Army as its has been replaced by the more recent RPG-7V.

The RPG-2 is a muzzle-loaded, shoulder-fired, smooth-bore, recoilless weapon and is recognisable by its long tube and its grip with a built-in firing trigger. It cannot be fired from the left shoulder as there is a gas escape hole on the RHS near the firing mechanism.

The RPG-2 is also built in Communist China as the Type 56 Anti-Tank Grenade Launcher and was designated B-40 by the North Vietnamese and Viet Cong. Its open sights are graduated for 50, 100 and

The Chinese Type 56 40mm anti-tank launcher compared with the original (lower) Soviet RPG-2 40mm anti-tank launcher.

150m. The weapon fires a PG-2 fin-stabilised HEAT grenade with a DK-4 base detonating fuse and a self-destruct mechanism. Earlier grenades had the DK-2 fuse which did not have the self-destruct feature. The PG-2 weighs 1.84kg and is 50cm in length, muzzle velocity is 84m/s and it will penetrate 18cm of armour.

If required the RPG-2 can be fitted with the NSP-2 infra-red night sight. Some models have been fitted with a modified blast deflector at the rear.

50mm Model M40 Mortar Soviet Union

Calibre: 50mm
Weight: 11.5kg
Length of barrel: 78.8cm
Elevation: +45° and +75°
Traverse: $5\frac{1}{2}$° (total)
Range: 807m at 45° elevation
129m at 75° elevation
Crew: 2-3

Before World War II, the Russians developed a series of lightweight 50mm mortars, these being designated the M38, M39, M40 and finally the M41. None of these is used by any of the Warsaw Pact Forces, but they are still used in some smaller countries and by some liberation forces.

The M40 was developed from the earlier M38 and it retained the earlier mortar's method of range adjustment. This is achieved by rotating a sleeve in the base of the mortar, this opened or closed a number of gas ports. To extend the range of the mortar the ports were all opened and to achieve the minimum range all of the ports were closed. The only type of mortar bomb available is a HE with just one charge.

94

9mm Super Star Pistol

Spain

Calibre: 9mm
Length: 20.4cm
Length of barrel: 13.3cm
Weight: 1.02kg
Mag capacity: 9 rounds
Muzzle velocity: 366m/s
Max effective range: 50m

Over the years the Spanish armament industry has produced a bewildering array of pistols in a very wide range of calibres and designs, many of them cheap copies of existing pistols. Among the better of the Spanish pistols have been the products of the firm of Star Bonifacio Echeverria SA Eibar, and one of their products, the 9mm Super Star is the current Spanish Army pistol. It combines some of the better design features of current American pistols and is a strong well-made weapon. Commercial versions have been sold in various calibres and are used by some police forces in several states.

9mm Star Model Z62 and Z-70/B Sub-Machine Guns

Spain

Calibre: 9mm
Length: 48cm (stock folded)
Length of barrel: 20.1cm
Weight: 3.55kg (loaded)
Mag capacity: 30 rounds
Muzzle velocity: 381m/s
Max effective range: 200m
Rate of fire: 550rpm (cyclic)

The Z62 is gradually replacing the earlier Z45 in service with the Spanish Army. It has several novel features including an involved safety mechanism that prevents firing if the weapon is dropped, and a 'half-moon' trigger that gives single shots when the lower part of the trigger is pulled and automatic when pressure is applied to the top half. In service this latter feature has proved troublesome and the later Model Z-70/B has had the mechanism replaced by a conventional trigger — the later model is identical to the earlier version in all other respects. In use, the Star SMGs have proved to be rugged and reliable weapons under a wide range of conditions.

9mm Star Model Z45 Sub-Machine Gun

Spain

Calibre: 9mm
Length: 57.9cm (stock folded)
Length of barrel: 19.8cm
Weight: 4.54kg (loaded)
Magazine capacity: 30 rounds
Muzzle velocity: 381m/s
Max effective range: 200m
Rate of fire: 450rpm (cyclic)

The Star Model Z45 was a Spanish design based on that of the German MP40 and was originally produced to a wartime German order. Production did not begin until mid-1944 and the weapon was issued to the Spanish Air Force and Civil Guard before being taken into service by the Spanish Army in 1949. The design differs from the MP40 in several respects, one of which is the barrel jacket, and the barrel which can be unscrewed from the front. Small numbers of this weapon were sold to Portugal, Cuba, Chile and Saudi Arabia. It is reported that some have been built in Indonesia.

7.62mm CETME Assault Rifles

Spain

Data: Model C
Calibre: 7.62mm
Length: 101.6cm
Length of barrel: 44.5cm
Weight: 4.48kg
Mag capacity: 20 rounds
Muzzle velocity: 762m/s
Rate of fire: 600rpm (cyclic)
120rpm (auto)
40rpm (single shot)

The first CETME 7.62mm assault rifle to go into production was the Model A, in 1956. This rifle had a development history going back to 1950 when a series of rifles, based on work carried out in France during the late 1940s (the weapon used as the basis was the World War II German 7.92mm StuG 45), was used to determine the form and mechanism that all later CETME rifles were to take. The round used was not the standard NATO round, although it had the same outward dimensions but a lower-powered cartridge known as the 'CETME-NATO'. The Model A

7.62mm CETME assault rifle Model B with bipod.

was followed in production by the Model B, in 1958 and this model was adopted by the Spanish armed forces in the same year. This model was also adopted by the West German forces and manufactured by Heckler and Koch as the G3. The next version was the Model C which uses standard NATO ammunition and this version also introduced some detail changes to the sights, muzzle and the bipod/wire-cutter became an optional extra. This model was adopted by the Spanish Air Force. Later versions were the Model D (Used for trials only) and the Model E which has provision for an optical sight and the use of plastic in place of wood on the furniture — a version with a retractable stock has been made but no production of the Model E has yet started. All the CETME rifles use the same roller-delay locking mechanism.

7.62mm CETME assault rifle Model E.

5.56mm CETME Model L Assault Rifle

Spain

Calibre: 5.56mm
Length: 92cm
Length of barrel: 40cm
Weight: 3.3kg (less mag)
Mag capacity: 10, 20 or 30 rounds
Muzzle velocity: 920m/s
Rate of fire: 750-800rpm (cyclic)

With the gradual changeover to smaller rifle calibre ammunition CETME developed their Model L in standard American 5.56mm. The Model L embodies a virtually unchanged CETME mechanism apart from weight and dimensional changes but embodied are all the features of the Model E. A controlled-burst feature is an extra mechanical fitting. The Model LC has a retractable butt.

Above: 5.56mm CETME Model L assault rifle.

Below: 5.56mm CETME Model LC assault rifle with butt retracted.

5.56mm CETME Machine Gun

Spain

Calibre: 5.56mm
Length: 93.5cm
Length of barrel: 40cm
Weight: 6.3kg (less bipod)
6.8kg (with bipod)
Type of feed: Belt
Muzzle velocity: 920m/s
Rate of fire: 1,000rpm

Although still experimental, this CETME machine gun is unusual in having a belt feed for 5.56mm ammunition. No other data is available.

5.56mm CETME machine gun with bipod.

3.5in Model 1965 Rocket Launcher Spain

Calibre: 3.5in (88.9mm)
Length: 160cm (operational)
83cm (folded)
Weight: 5.4kg
Range: 450m
Crew: 1-2

This weapon is a further development of the Model 1953 and 1958 launchers which were based on the American M20 rocket launcher. The Model 1965 is built in Spain by Instalaza SA of Zaragoza, and is in service with the Spanish Army.

The firing mechanism is electric and the circuit is completed when a rocket is inserted into the barrel. The aiming mechanism consists of an elevating device and an optical sight. A regulator with two scales is positioned on the elevating device, one for anti-tank rounds with settings to 2,500m and the other for HE and smoke rounds with settings to 1,500m. The optical sight has a reticle engraved with elevation to 650m range. There are three types of rocket available for the Model 1965 and all are fin-stabilised; they are issued in watertight plastic containers which float. The American M20-series launchers can be modified to fire these rockets.

HEAT Rocket CH M65
Weight: 2kg
Muzzle velocity: 230m/s
Max range: 2,500m
Armour penetration: 33cm
Concrete penetration: 80cm

HE Rocket MB 66
Weight: 3.1kg
Muzzle velocity: 155m/s
Max range: 1,500m
Armour penetration: 25cm
Concrete penetration: 70cm

Incendiary Smoke FI M66
Weight: 2.7kg
Muzzle velocity: 155m/s
Max range: 1,500m

60mm ECIA Commando Mortar Spain

Calibre: 60.7mm
Weight: 5.9kg
3.1kg (barrel and breech)
2.8kg (baseplate)
Length of barrel: 65cm
Range: 1,070m
Rate of fire: 30rpm (max)
Crew: 2 (1 man can carry the mortar complete)

This light mortar basically consists of a barrel and a very small baseplate. The weapon can be held by one hand (the left) and the mortar bomb dropped in with the other. There is a canvas sleeve around the middle of the mortar's barrel to protect the hand from heat. A simple sight is provided. Ammunition used is the same as that used for the ECIA 60mm Mortar Model L.

The ECIA 60mm Commando mortar.

60mm ECIA Model L Mortar

Spain

Calibre: 60.7mm
Weight: 12kg (total)
4.2kg (barrel and breech piece)
2.8kg (baseplate)
3.9kg (mount)
1.1kg (sight)
Length of barrel: 65cm
Range: 1,975m
Rate of fire: 30rpm
Crew: 2 (1 man can carry the complete mortar)

This mortar is manufactured by Esperanza Y Cia SA of Spain and is in service with the Spanish Army.

The mortar consists of a steel barrel, breech piece with a trigger mechanism, baseplate, sight and tripod. The two unusual features of this mortar are its tripod (most mortars have a bipod) and its trigger which allows it to be fired either in the normal way (ie by gravity) or by trigger action.

The following types of ammunition have been developed for both the 60mm mortar Model L and the 60mm Commando mortar — HE and High Capacity HE Bombs and illuminating, smoke and practice bombs. There are a total of five charges. The HE Bomb is 26.3cm in length and weighs 1.43kg, it has a filling of .232kg of TNT and its maximum effective radius is 50m.

The ECIA 60mm Model L mortar in the firing position.

9mm m/45 Sub-Machine Gun

Sweden

Calibre: 9mm
Length: 80.8cm (stock extended)
55.2cm (stock folded)
Length of barrel: 21cm
Weight: 5kg (loaded)
Mag capacity: 36 rounds
Muzzle velocity: 420m/s
Max effective range: 200m
Rate of fire: 550-600rpm (cyclic)

Usually known as the 'Carl Gustav' and not to be confused with the rocket launcher of the same name (qv), the m/45 was first produced in 1945 and is still in production. Its correct Swedish designation is the 9mm k-pist (the latter being an abbreviation for kulsprutepistol). It is the standard Swedish sub-machine gun and has been sold widely — Indonesia and Eire have been customers and the model was produced for a while in Egypt as the 'Port Said'. One version is the m/45B which can take a special 36-round wedge-shaped box magazine as well as the original 50-round box magazine adopted from the Finnish Suomi m/37-39, but the later models will

The 9mm m/45 Carl Gustav SMG.

accept only the 36-round magazine. The m/45 fires a special 9mm round with a thick jacket to increase penetration.

A silenced version of the m/45 was produced and used by American Special Forces in South-East Asia.

The Swedish firm of Husqvarna carried out some further development to the basic m/45 which resulted in the Hovea M49. This sub-machine gun is still used by the Danish Army and is essentially similar in most respects to the m/45.

5.56mm MKS Assault Rifle Sweden

	MKS RIFLE	MKS CARBINE
Calibre:	5.56mm	5.56mm
Length (overall):	86.8cm	75.1cm
Length (stock folded):	63.4cm	51.7cm
Length of barrel:	46.7cm	35cm
Weight (with mag and sling):	3.36kg	2.97kg
Weight (without mag):	2.75kg	2.36kg
Mag capacity:	30	30
Range:	400m	400m
Muzzle velocity:	975m/s	925m/s
Rate of fire:	700rpm (cyclic)	700rpm (cyclic)

The MKS has been developed by a new Swedish Company called Interdynamic AB of Stockholm. It has been designed specifically for export as the Swedish Army does not intend to adopt the small 5.56mm round at the present time. It has been designed for easy manufacture and extensive use is made of sheet metal components and moulded plastic.

The MKS uses the standard 5.56mm cartridge and fires from the closed bolt; it is gas-operated. The magazine is housed in the pistol grip and the stock can be folded through 180° so that it lays alongside the weapon. The barrel is provided with a combined flash-eliminator and grenade launcher; a bayonet can be fitted if required.

Either single shots or bursts can be selected. The fore sight is of the hooded post type and the rear sight can be adjusted for both 250 and 400m ranges. Interdynamic is now developing a micro-calibre, low recoil, burst rifle called the MKR. This will have a large capacity magazine and a range of over 300m.

Below: The 5.56mm MKS rifle.

Bottom: The 5.56mm MKS carbine.

6.5mm Ljungman Rifles

Sweden

Calibre: 6.5mm
Length: 21.4cm
Length of barrel: 62.2cm
Weight: 4.71kg (empty)
Mag capacity: 10 rounds
Muzzle velocity: 750m/s
Max effective range: 600m
Rate of fire: 60rpm (single shot)

The first of the Ljungman semi-automatic rifles was designed in 1942 and entered service with the Swedish Army in late 1942 as the *halvautomatisk gevar 42*. It was the first automatic rifle to see large scale service with any army and embodied a number of design features that have since been incorporated in such models as the Armalite AR-10 and AR-15. In 1953 some changes were made to produce the *halvautomatisk gevar 42B* (AG 42B). Both versions were produced by the Danish Madsen concern and a 7.92mm version was produced in Egypt as the 'Hakim' rifle. The AG 42B has now passed from first-line Swedish service and is used only by second-line and reserve units. It has been replaced by a locally-produced version of the Heckler and Koch G3, the AK-4.

84mm Carl-Gustaf M2 Rocket Launcher

Sweden

Calibre: 84mm
Weight: 29.5kg (packed gun and accessories)
14.2kg (gun)
.8kg (mount)
1kg (telescopic sight)
Length: 113cm
Range: 400m (HEAT round moving target)
500m (HEAT round stationary target)
1,000m (HE round)
1,000m (smoke round)
2,000m (illuminating round)
Rate of fire: 6rpm
Crew: 2

The Carl-Gustaf is manufactured by FFV of Sweden and has been adopted by many countries. Although primarily an anti-tank weapon various other types of ammunition have been developed which make the Carl-Gustaf a very useful infantry support weapon. The normal crew is two men, one carries the launcher, and the other carries 8 rounds of ammunition.

The Carl-Gustaf M2-550 84mm rocket launcher complete with sights.

The Carl-Gustaf is breech-loaded and percussion-fired. The round is fired by a side primer and the venturi is opened and closed with a rotary movement. The venturi must be in the closed position and locked by the fastening strap before the launcher can be fired.

The telescopic sight is mounted on the LHS of the weapon and has a ×2 magnification and a 17° field of view. Luminous fore and rear sight adapters are available for use during night firing.

The following types of ammunition are available for the Carl-Gustaf:

FFV 65 HEAT Round: This weighs 2.6kg and will penetrate 40cm of armour, time of flight to 300m = 1.2sec; it has an electric fuse.

FFV 441 HE Round: Weight 3.1kg, time of flight to 700m = 3.4sec, can be fitted with an impact or air-burst fuse.

FFV 469 Smoke Round: Weight 3.1kg, impact fuse and an instant smokescreen.

FFV 545 Illuminating Round: Weight 3.1kg, has a burning time of 30sec and will illuminate an area of 400-500m in diameter, 650,000 candelas.

For training there is an inert-filled Target Practice Tracer Projectile (TPT) which is the counterpart of the HEAT round. There is also a 6.5mm sub-calibre adapter for practice training.

Anti-Tank System FFV 550 (84mm Carl-Gustaf M2-550)

The FFV 550 is basically the standard M2 fitted with the new FFV 555 Sight and fires the new FFV 551 round. The FFV 555 Sight is an optical-electronic sighting system by means of which range and lead can be determined. This comprises a telescope, range-finder, and a lead-finder. The sight has a maximum range of 1,000m and weighs 3.4kg; it has a ×3 magnification and a 12° field of view.

FFV 551 HEAT Round: This round has been developed for use with the above sight. The complete round weighs 3kg with the projectile weighing 2.2kg. Maximum range is at least 700m which is achieved by a rocket motor starting after the shell has left the barrel. Muzzle velocity is 290m/s and maximum velocity is 380m/s. Time of flight to 400m is 1.2sec and to 700m, 2.1sec. This round will penetrate 70cm of armour. There is also a 7.62mm sub-calibre adapter for use with the FFV 550 System.

The Carl-Gustaf M2 84mm Rocket Launcher of Austrian Army in action.

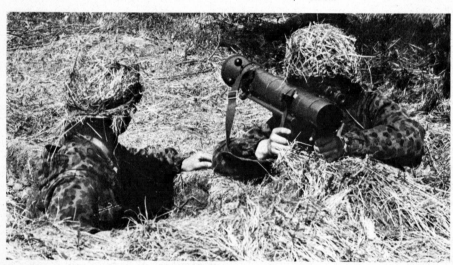

74mm Miniman Anti-Tank Launcher Sweden

Calibre: 74mm
Length: 90cm (total)
Weight: 2.9kg (total)
Range: 250m (stationary target)
150m (moving target)
Crew: 1 or 2

The Miniman is a lightweight recoilless weapon that can be used against both tanks and fortifications. The weapon is pre-loaded and instantly prepared for firing by removing the muzzle cover, erecting the sights and cocking the mechanical firing mechanism. Once the weapon is fired the Miniman is discarded. The HEAT shell weighs .88kg, has a muzzle velocity of 160m/s and will penetrate 34cm of armour. The shell is not armed until it is approx 10m from the muzzle of the weapon and is stabilised in flight by fins.

The barrel is made of glass-fibre reinforced plastic, the sights and firing mechanism are also of plastic and are bonded to the barrel. The combustion chamber is of high-strength aluminium alloy. The Miniman is waterproof and is normally carried by a sling. A waterproof package is also available which carries two Miniman weapons, this is made of polystyrene with a covering of aluminium and will float if dropped in water. A 9mm sub-calibre training device has been developed for the Miniman.

SIG Pistols Switzerland

Data: SIG P-210
Calibre: 9mm
Length: 21.6cm
Length of barrel: 12cm
Weight: .909kg (empty)
Mag capacity: 8 rounds
Muzzle velocity: 335m/s
Range: 50m

The P-210 is manufactured by SIG in four basic models:
P-210-1: 12cm barrel for military and police duties, 9mm or 7.65mm calibre.
P-210-2: 12cm barrel for military and police duties, 9mm or 7.65mm calibre.
P-210-5: 15cm barrel for target shooting.
P-210-6: 12cm barrel for target shooting

The SIG 210-2 pistol.

If required the P-210-1/2 can be converted to .22in calibre. The system of operation is of the short recoil type. The difference between the 2-210-1 and P-210-2 is that the P-210-1 has a polished finish whilst the P-210-2 has a sandblasted finish and is provided with a lanyard loop. Its fore sight is of the blade type and its rear sight is of the notch type. The P-210-2 is used by a number of armed forces including Switzerland and Denmark.

The P220 pistol.

The P230 pistol.

Recently SIG have entered into an agreement with JP Sauer and the following pistols have recently entered production:
P220 which is available in .45in, .38in and 9mm and can be converted to .22in calibre.
P230 which is available in 9mm or 7.65mm models and can also be converted to .22in calibre with a simple kit.

SIG 540, SIG 542 and SIG 543 Automatic Rifles
Switzerland

	SIG 540	SIG 542
Calibre:	5.56mm	7.62mm
Length: overall	95cm	100.2cm
butt folded	71.4cm	74.8cm
Length of barrel:	49cm	49.5cm
Weight: with fixed butt		
without bipod and mag	3.12kg	3.36kg
with bipod	3.54kg	3.86kg
Mag capacity:	20 rounds	20 or
		30 rounds
Range:	400m	400m
Rate of fire: cyclic	650/800rpm	650/800rpm
auto	90rpm	80rpm
single shots	40rpm	40rpm

Some years ago SIG developed a weapon called the SIG 530-1 in 5.56mm calibre, both long and short barrelled models were built as were both fixed and folding-stock models, none of these, however, went into production.

The SIG 540 and SIG 543 fire the 5.56mm × 45mm cartridge with a m/v of 980m/s whilst the SIG 542 fires the 7.62mm × 51mm cartridge with a m/v of 820m/s.

The weapons are gas-operated with a rotating bolt. The fore sight is of the cylindrical post type whilst the rear sight is of the aperture type. The SIG 540, SIG 543 graduated from 100 to 500m and the SIG 542 from 100 to 600m. It is available with a fixed stock or a folding butt; a bipod can be provided. Optional equipment includes a bayonet, telescopic sight, night sight and a three-round burst control device.

The SIG 542 automatic rifle with bipod and telescopic sight.

7.62mm SIG 510-4 Automatic Rifle   Switzerland

Calibre: 7.62mm
Length: 101.5cm
Length of barrel: 50.5cm
Weight: 4.25kg (gun only)
4.56kg (with bipod)
Mag capacity: 20 rounds
Range: 600m
Rate of fire: 60rpm (cyclic)
80rpm (auto)
40rpm (single shots)

The standard rifle of the Swiss Army is the SIG built AM55 (StGW57). The SIG 510 series were developed from the earlier weapon and there are the following models in the range:
SIG 510-1 for 7.62mm × 51mm NATO round
SIG 510-2 for 7.62mm × 51mm NATO round (lighter model)
SIG 510-3 for the 7.62mm × 39mm Soviet round
SIG 510-4 for the 7.62mm × 51mm NATO round; there is also a sporting model called the SG-AMT.

The SIG 510-4 7.62mm automatic rifle complete with bipod.

The SIG 510-4 is the only member of the family that has been sold in any great quantity and most of these have gone to South America (including Bolivia and Chile). The weapon's system of operation is of the delayed blowback type with a semi-rigid breech. It has a selector for single shot or full automatic and a bipod is provided.

The rear sight is of the aperture type and the front sight is of the cylindrical post type; the rear sight is graduated from 100 to 600m in 100m increments. On the SIG 510-3 it is sighted to 500m only.

A wide range of accessories are available including a ×4 telescope, sling, bayonet and night sight. Anti-tank grenades can be fired from this weapon.

7.51mm M-31 (Schmidt-Rubin) Rifle   Switzerland
7.51mm M-31/55 Sniper's Rifle

	M-31	M-31/55
Calibre:	7.51mm	7.51mm
Length:	110.4cm	121cm
Length of barrel:	65.2cm	65.5cm
Weight:	4.01kg	5.53kg
Mag capacity:	6	6
Muzzle velocity:	780m/s	—
Range:	400m	400/600m
Rate of fire:	12rpm	12rpm

In 1889, two men, Colonel Schmidt and Colonel Rubin, developed a rifle which became known as the Model 1889 and this was adopted by the Swiss Army. After this came the Model 1889/96, the Model M1897 which was a single-shot rifle for training purposes, the Model 89/00 was a shorter model for the use of fortress troops, the M1905 was

a light carbine model whilst the Model 1896/11 was chambered for the M1911 cartridge. The next model was the M-31 (or K-31 = Karabiner 31).

The M1931/42 was a sniper's rifle with a telescope, magnification ×1.8, the M1931/48 was a sniper's rifle with a telescope, magnification ×2.8. The current sniper's rifle is known as the M1935/55 and is provided with a telescope, magnification of ×3.5, a muzzle brake, and a bipod.

The 7.51mm M-31 Schmidt-Rubin rifle.

7.51mm MG51 Machine Gun   Switzerland

Calibre: 7.51mm
Length: 127cm
Length of barrel: 56.4cm
Weight: 15.8kg
27kg (with tripod)
Range: 1,000m (with tripod)
Rate of fire: 1,000rpm

The MG51 (Maschinengewehr Model 1961) is the standard machine gun of the Swiss Army. The

weapon can be used with either a bipod or a tripod. When being used with the latter the bipod is folded up underneath the barrel. Ammunition is in belts of 250.

The Swiss Army also used a light machine gun called the LMG 25 (Leichtes Maschinengewehr 25); this is fed from a 30-round magazine on the RHS. Its cyclic rate of fire is 450rpm, and its maximum effective range is 800m. The weapon is normally used with a bipod although a tripod is also available.

7.62mm SIG 710-3 Machine Gun   Switzerland

Calibre: 7.62mm
Length: 114.6cm
Length of barrel: 56cm
Weight: 9.65kg (gun)
.7kg (bipod)
2kg (standard barrel)
2.3kg (heavy barrel)
10.2kg (tripod)
Range: 2,200m (tripod)
800m (bipod)
Rate of fire: 800/900rpm (cyclic)
200/300rpm (auto)

The 7.62mm 710-3 machine gun was designed over 10 years ago by SIG of Neuhausen Rhine Falls. To date, however, it has not been produced in large quantities. It can be used in both the LMG role with a bipod or in the heavy role with a tripod and a heavy

barrel. It can be fitted with an ammunition box holding 100 rounds.

It fires a standard NATO cartridge with a m/v of 790m/s. System of operation is delayed blow-back with stationary barrel and semi-rigid roller type breech. Ammunition is fed from the left via steel belts or disintegrating belts.

The fore sight is of the protected blade type and the rear sight is of leaf type graduated from 100 to 1,200m in increments of 100m. Early models had a wooden butt, but more recent models have a metal stock.

A wide range of accessories are available including a ×2.5 telescopic sight, infra-red night sight, and a tripod mount.

The SIG 7.62mm 710-3 machine gun on L810 Tripod.

83mm M58 Anti-Tank Weapon Switzerland

Calibre: 83mm
Weight: 7.5kg (empty)
Length: 130cm
Effective range: 200m
Crew: 1-2

This Swiss-designed weapon is known as the 8.3cm Raketenrohr 58 by the Swiss Army. It fires a round

weighing 1.82kg with a muzzle velocity of 200m/s. It is provided with a shield which has a sighting window to protect the operator when the weapon is fired. The latest model is called the M-75 which fires a fin-stabilised projectile to a range of 400-500m.

American Revolvers

Although there are now no revolvers still in use with the American forces, so many thousands have been produced over the years that it would be futile to suggest that any one of the numerous models produced is no longer in military service. By its very nature the revolver is sturdy and efficient and requires less maintenance than its automatic counterpart. As a result, in many places the revolver is still used by military police, rear-echelon and para-military forces. Space precludes a complete breakdown of all the American types still in use and mention of the American revolvers has been limited to a listing of the types most likely still to be encountered:

Smith & Wesson .38in /200
Smith & Wesson Hand Ejector Revolver M1917

Smith & Wesson .38in Model No 10
Smith & Wesson .38in Model No 12
Smith & Wesson .38in Model No 15
Smith & Wesson .38in Model No 37 and 38 'Air-weight'
Colt .45in New Service M1917
Colt .38in Agent
Colt .38in Police Special
Colt .38in or .357in Magnum Mark 111 Lawman

This list is by no means fully comprehensive but merely gives an idea of the types likely to be in service. Note that as a general rule the super-powerful Magnum rounds have yet to be fully accepted as service issue although they are widely used by law enforcement agencies and may therefore be used by military police units.

.45in M1911 and M1911A1 Automatic Pistol United States

The .45in M1911A1 automatic pistol.

Calibre: .45in (11.43mm)
Length: 21.91cm
Length of barrel: 12.78cm
Weight: 1.36kg (loaded)
1.13kg (empty)
Mag capacity: 7 rounds
Muzzle velocity: 252m/s
Max effective range: 20m

The Colt M1911 was taken into US Army service in 1911 and in 1926 some changes were made to the basic design to produce the M1911A1. Today, both models are still in service with the US forces and with numerous other armies all round the world, as well as many police and para-military formations. It has been licence-built by several nations (such as Norway) and has been used as the basis for myriad copy models (many Spanish pistols are still based on the M1911 or M1911A1). By now both models have been produced and issued in tens of thousands by several American firms. The standard bullet fired is a 230g projectile (.45in Ball M1911) but recently several other types of ammunition have been developed especially for police forces — these include hollow-headed bullets and specially-shaped Teflon-coated projectiles for use against metal-bodied vehicles. The conventional ball round has prodigious man-stopping qualities but the heavy recoil makes the pistol rather awkward to handle with accuracy and careful training is needed to use both models effectively.

Ingram M-10 Sub-Machine Guns   United States

*The Ingram M-11
SMG with silencer.*

Muzzle velocity: 280m/s (.45in)
366m/s (9mm)
Max effective range: 100m
Rate of fire (.45in): 1,145rpm (cyclic)
90rpm (auto)
40rpm (single shots)

Calibre: .45in (11.43mm) or 9mm
Length: 54.8cm (stock extended)
26.9cm (stock retracted)
26.7cm (no stock)
Length of barrel: 14.6cm
Weight: 3.82kg (loaded, 30 rounds)
2.84kg (empty)
Mag capacity: 30 or 32 rounds

Gordon B. Ingram has designed and produced a number of SMGs since 1945. His Model 6 was produced for various American police forces, the Cuban Navy and for Peru, but subsequent models did not do so well until Ingram produced the Model 10 in 1970. The Model 10 has obvious affinities with the Uzi SMG but the construction methods are different and the M-10 is much smaller. Because of the light bolt, the rate of fire of the M-10 is high but it is intended for firing in short bursts only. Despite an energetic sales campaign the M-10 has been sold only to Chile and Yugoslavia although many countries have bought trial batches and many police forces now use some for law enforcement. The M-10 can be bought in .45in or 9mm calibre and a smaller lighter version, the M-11, is available in .38in calibre. Production is now undertaken by RPB Industries Inc of Atlanta, Georgia.

Ingram LR Sub-Machine Gun   United States

Calibre: 9mm or .45in
Length: 83cm (stock extended)
64cm (stock retracted)
Length of barrel: 45cm
Weight: 4.316kg (loaded mag)
3.635kg (without mag)
Mag capacity: 32 rounds of 9mm
30 rounds of .45in
Effective range: 200m
Rate of fire: 1,090rpm (cyclic)

The Ingram LR sub-machine gun is basically the Ingram sub-machine gun body, pistol grip and magazine with a longer barrel chambered for pistol

ammunition. The standard metal telescopic stock can be replaced by a wooden stock if required. The weapon is blowback operated and the firer can select either semi- or full automatic. The fore sight is of the hooded post type with the rear sight being adjustable from 50 to 350m. The Ingram LR sub-machine gun is currently in production for export only.

.45in M3 and M3A1 Sub-Machine Guns United States

Calibre: .45in (11.43mm) and 9mm
Length: 75.7cm (stock extended)
57.9cm (stock retracted)
Length of barrel: 20.3cm
Weight: 4.52kg (M3A1 loaded and complete)
Mag capacity: 30 rounds
Muzzle velocity: 280m/s
Max effective range: 200m
Rate of fire: 450rpm (cyclic)
120rpm (auto)

When America entered the war in 1941 there was a shortage of SMGs and the Thompson was proving difficult to mass-produce. The example of the British Sten and German MP40 was taken as the starting point of what became the M3 sub-machine gun, a simple all-metal weapon designed for easy and cheap production. The M3 was produced in very large numbers and was replaced in production by the M3A1 which was an even simpler design in which the cocking handle was replaced by a finger hole in the breech block. The M3A1 was kept in production until the Korean War and many were distributed to Taiwan and the Philippines and many more were sold to South American countries. Many of the Far East examples are in 9mm calibre. The basic M3 design has been extensively copied 'unofficially' — typical examples are the Argentinian PAM 1 and 2 in 9mm, and the Chinese Type 36 (.45in and 37 (9mm).

The .45in M3A1 SMG which was also known as the 'grease gun'.

Thompson Sub-Machine Guns United States

Data: M1928A1
Calibre: .45in (11.43mm)
Length: 85.2cm (overall)
63.5cm (minus butt)
Weight: 5.63kg (loaded 30 rounds)
4.9kg (empty)
Mag capacity: 20- or 30-round box
50-round drum
Muzzle velocity: 282m/s
Max effective range: 200m
Rate of fire: 700rpm (cyclic)
120rpm (auto)
40rpm (single shots)

The Thompson sub-machine gun was the first American sub-machine gun, and development started during World War I. The first model was the Model 1921 but production and sales were slow despite a number of design changes and the impetus

given by the 'gangster era'. The first true military model was the M1928A1 which was standardised in 1938, and war production produced the M1 and M1A1. These last two models were produced by the thousand despite the unsuitability of the Thompson for mass-production. In service the Thompson proved bulky and rather complex to maintain but it was used all over the world and gained a formidable reputation as a close-combat gun. After 1945 its cost and weight were the deciding factors in its being replaced by more modern weapons and today the Thompson has almost entirely vanished from the military scene. It remains in small-scale service in Egypt, Haiti and Yugoslavia, and many have found their way into the hands of the IRA. Numerous 'unofficial' copies have been made by some small countries, typical of which are the crude copies made in China and used in Vietnam.

5.56mm Ruger Mini-14 Rifle   United States

Calibre: 5.56mm
Length: 94.6cm
Length of barrel: 47cm
Weight: 3.1kg (loaded 20 rounds)
2.9kg (empty)
Mag capacity: 5, 20 or 30 rounds
Muzzle velocity: 1,005m/s
Max effective range: 300m
Rate of fire: 40rpm (semi-auto)

With the Mini-14 rifle, Ruger have made a return to 'conventional' firearm construction while at the same time using the modern small-calibre 5.56mm round. The action is basically that of the M1 Garand rifle

scaled down to suit the new cartridge. This action has been retained as it has proved strong and reliable over the years and the Mini-14 is designed for a long life and rugged treatment. The stock is made from hardwood in a style not seen in military firearms for some years and the metal used for the mechanism and receiver is high-grade steel. Ammunition can be either the 5.56mm × .45in cartridge or any commercial equivalent. As yet the Ruger Mini-14 has been purchased by few military buyers but its sound construction means it should be a very attractive proposition for many armies.

The 5.56mm Ruger MINI-14 rifle.

5.56mm Armalite AR-18 Rifle   United States

Calibre: 5.56mm
Length: 94cm (stock extended)
73.6cm (stock folded)

Length of barrel: 47.6cm
Weight: 3.58kg (loaded)
Mag capacity: 20 rounds

Muzzle velocity: 990m/s
Max effective range: 400m
Rate of fire: 750-800rpm (cyclic)
80rpm (auto)
40rpm (single shots)

The AR-18 is a development of the AR-15 which has been carried out by Armalite to produce a modern weapon which can be fabricated and assembled by relatively simple and cheap machinery. The AR-15 for all its advantages requires relatively complex and expensive production facilities and in many parts of the world these are not available. The AR-18 therefore makes use of metal stampings, welding,

The AR-18.

and plastic where possible. Although not accepted for use by the US Army, the AR-18 has been extensively tested by them. Production is under way by Armalites at Costa Mesa in California, in Japan, and in the UK by the Sterling Armament Company. As well as the basic AR-18, two other models are available — the AR-18S which is a shortened SMG version, and the AR-180 which an fire semi-automatic only and cannot be easily converted for full automatic fire.

The AR-18 with stock folded back.

5.56mm Stoner 63 System

United States

Calibre: 5.56mm
Length: 102.2cm
Length of barrel: 50.8cm
Weight: 4.39kg (with 30 rounds)
3.51kg (weapon only)
Range: 400m

Muzzle velocity: 1,000m/s
Rate of fire: 600rpm (cyclic)
90rpm (auto)
40rpm (single shots)

The Stoner 63 Assault Rifle.

The Stoner 63 system was designed by the Cadillac Gage Company, the first prototypes being completed in 1962. These were chambered for the standard 7:62mm × 51mm NATO cartridge. There followed a model chambered for the 5.56mm × 45mm cartridge and this round was subsequently adopted for the complete range of weapons.

The system itself is designed around the same receiver, bolt and piston, return spring, trigger and firing mechanism. From those components the following could be built up — sub-machine gun, assault rifle, light machine gun (belt fed), light machine gun (magazine fed), medium machine gun and a machine gun suitable for installation in armoured vehicles.

The weapons are gas-operated and system of locking is of the rotating bolt type. The fore sight is of the cylindrical post type and the rear sight is of the flip aperture type.

The LMG was used in Vietnam by the United States Marine Corps as the XM207. The other components of the system have not been produced in quantity although licences were issued to the Dutch company of NWM.

5.56mm Colt Commando Rifle   United States

Calibre: 5.56mm
Length: 78.7cm (butt extended)
71.1cm (butt retracted)
Length of barrel: 25.4cm
Weight: 3.23kg (loaded)
Mag capacity: 20 or 30 rounds
Muzzle velocity: 824m/s
Max effective range: 200m
Rate of fire: 700-800rpm (cyclic)
150-200rpm (auto)
40-50rpm (single shots)

The Colt Commando is a shortened version of the M16 rifle (qv) developed for use in the jungles of SE Asia and in most details, apart from the length is identical to the M16 in handling, appearance and mechanism. It has been used in action in Vietnam by special forces under the designation of XM177E2, but at present its future is uncertain. Accuracy and handling when fired tend to be impaired by the short barrel.

The 5.56mm Colt Commando.

5.56mm M16 and M16A1 Rifles   United States

Calibre: 5.56mm
Length: 99cm (with flash suppressor)
Length of barrel: 50.8cm
Weight: 3.82kg (M16A1 loaded 30 rounds)
3.18kg (M16A1 empty)
Mag capacity: 20 or 30 rounds
Muzzle velocity: 990m/s
Max effective range: 400m
Rate of fire: 700-950rpm (cyclic)
150-200rpm (auto)
45-65rpm (semi-auto)

The M16 rifle is the Armalite AR-15 designed by Eugene Stoner and is a logical development of the AR-10. Using the smaller 5.56mm × 45mm cartridge, the AR-15 is a much smaller and lighter weapon than its predecessor and thus has definite handling, supply and 'handiness' advantages. The US Air Force was first to obtain the AR-15 as the M16 and the US Army then bought the type as the M16A1 which differs in having a bolt closure plunger on the RHS of the receiver. The M16A1 is now the standard rifle of the US Army and to date well over 5,000,000 have been produced. The M16A1 was introduced into service when the US Army was in action in Vietnam and many early troubles arose from inadequate training and changes in the ammunition specification. These troubles were,

The 5.56mm M16A1 complete with bipod.

however, eradicated and the M16 series is now a reliable service weapon. It has been widely exported and is licence-built in Singapore, South Korea and the Philippines. The UK has bought a small batch for use in the Far East and by Ghurka units. Many Far East nations have bought the M16 as its light weight and small size make it ideal for handling by the small-statured races of that part of the world. Other user nations are Jordan, Taiwan and Italy (special service units only).

The M16 and M16A1 are manufactured by Colt Fire Arms Inc, although some have been made by Harrington and Richardson, and the Hydramatic Division of General Motors. The weapon is also manufactured under licence in Philippines, Singapore and South Korea. The mechanism is gas-operated and fire can be full automatic or semi-automatic. A bipod can be fitted, as can a bayonet. The flash suppressor, which is fixed, can be used to fire standard rifle grenades. An extra attachment is the M203 40mm grenade launcher which fits below the barrel (replacing the earlier M79 grenade launcher). The M203 fires one shot at a time and has a maximum range of 350m, although its effective range is 150-200m. A wide variety of ammunition is available for the M203 including HE, fragmentation, armour piercing and illuminating.

Below: Colt M16 fitted with Laser Lok sight.

Bottom: M203 40mm Grenade Launcher attachment mounted on a standard M16A1 rifle.

7.62mm AR-10 Assault Rifle

United States

Calibre: 7.62mm
Length: 102.9cm
Length of barrel: 50.8cm
Weight: 4.82kg (loaded)
4.24kg (empty)
Mag capacity: 20 rounds
Muzzle velocity: 845m/s
Max effective range: 500m
Rate of fire: 700rpm (cyclic)
80rpm (auto)
40rpm (single shots)

The Armalite AR-10 was produced originally as an assault rifle in .30in calibre but this was soon changed to accommodate the 7.62mm × 51mm NATO cartridge. There were many design features built into the AR-10 that were later to be incorporated into the AR-15 but the AR-10 had little commercial success as it was brought out at the time of the move away from the 7.62mm calibre to the smaller 5.56mm. Plans to produce the weapon in Holland came to nothing and the only sales were of small batches to the Sudan, Burma, Portugal and Nicaragua. Trial models of the AR-10 were produced as light machine guns using either magazine or belt feeds. A carbine model was also made. None of these trial models were produced for sale, but many features were designed into later Armalite products.

The AR-10 7.62mm assault rifle.

7.62mm M14A1 Rifle

United States

Calibre: 7.62mm
Length: 112cm (overall)
Length of barrel: 55.9cm
Weight: 6.6kg (loaded)
Mag capacity: 20 rounds
Muzzle velocity: 853m/s
Max effective range: 700m (with bipod)
460m (without bipod)
Rate of fire: 700-750rpm (cyclic)
60rpm (auto)
40rpm (single shots)

The M1 Garand rifle served the American forces well but its weight and small magazine were held to be undesirable features by the early 1950s and much experimental work went on to produce a lighter, full automatic version. When the 7.62mm × 51mm

NATO round was selected in 1953, a new rifle based on the Garand was adopted. This rifle had a long development history and was selected for production as the M14. This was basically a Garand mechanism updated to give automatic fire and in 1968 the M14A1 went into production with better facilities for full automatic fire, including a bipod. The M14 and M14A1 had a relatively short front-line service life despite the fact that about 1,500,000 were produced. It is now relegated to National Guard units, but one variant, the Rifle 7.62mm M21, is still in use as a specialist sniper rifle. The M21 is carefully assembled and fires only match ammunition. Many M-14 and M14A1 rifles are still in use around the world and the type has been licence built in Taiwan. Nations using the M14 include South Korea and the type was also used by South Vietnam.

.30in M1 Carbine United States

Calibre: .30in (7.62mm)
Length: 90.4cm (M1)
90.5cm (M1A1 stock extended)
64.8cm (M1A1 stock folded)
Length of barrel: 45.8cm
Weight: 2.63kg (M1 loaded)
2.77kg (M1A1 loaded)
2.63kg (M2 loaded)
Mag capacity: 15 or 30 rounds
Muzzle velocity: 607m/s
Max effective range: 300m
Rate of fire (M2): 750rpm (cyclic)
75rpm (auto)
40rpm (single shots)

The M1 carbine was designed by Winchester in 1940 and 1941 in answer to a call for a light rifle to replace the pistol in rear echelon units and increase their potential fire power. It went into production in

late 1941 and by the time production ceased well over 6,000,000 had been made. The basic M1 was a semi-automatic weapon and the M1A1 had a folding stock. A later version, the M2, was capable of automatic fire, and a further version, the M3 was a special 'sniper' variant. There were numerous other experimental versions but few went into service. The M1 and M2 were eventually issued to front-line combat units for use by officers and NCOs, but has now been largely replaced by the M-16 with the American forces except for some National Guard units. The M2 remains in service in Ethiopia, Chile, Taiwan, Honduras, Japan, Cambodia, South Korea, Laos, Mexico, Norway, the Philippines and Tunisia. The M1 and M2 have been produced under licence by Beretta for the Italian Army as the Model 1957 (also sold to Morocco), and have been copied in Dominica as the Cristobal Carbine M2.

.30in M1 (Garand) Rifle United States

Calibre: .30in (7.62mm)
Length: 110.7cm
Length of barrel: 61cm
Weight: 4.3kg (empty)
Mag capacity: 8 rounds
Muzzle velocity: 865m/s
Max effective range: 600m

The M1 rifle, often referred to as the Garand after its designer, was adopted as standard for the US forces in 1932. Production began in 1937 and did not end until the mid-1950s by which time about 5,500,000 had been made. The M1 was the first semi-automatic rifle to be selected for service and although numerous experimental versions were made the basic design remained unchanged throughout its service life. The rifle is loaded with an eight-round clip — single round loading is not possible — and the mechanism is gas-operated. Since 1945 the M1 has been issued or sold to many nations, and one, Italy, has produced the M1 under licence for the Italian Army as the Fucile M-1 Garand (some of these have been rechambered for the 7.62mm NATO round). Among user nations are

The.30in M1D (Garand) rifle.

Chile, Taiwan, Costa Rica, Denmark (m/50), Greece, Guatemala, Haiti, Indonesia, Iran, Japan, Jordan, Mexico, Norway, the Philippines, Tunisia, Turkey and Honduras. Although no longer in front-line American service the M1 is still in use by some National Guard units.

.30in Browning Automatic Rifle United States

Data: M1918A2
Calibre: .30in (7.62mm)
Length: 121.5cm
Length of barrel: 61cm
Weight: 8.82kg (empty)
Mag capacity: 20 rounds
Muzzle velocity: 860m/s
Max effective range: 600m
Rate of fire: 550rpm (cyclic)
350rpm (slow auto)

The Browning Automatic Rifle, or BAR, can be regarded as either a heavy automatic rifle or a rather light LMG. Since its introduction into US Army service in 1918 it was used as a squad fire support weapon and remained in use with the Americans

until well into the 1960s — the last production models were made during the Korean War. There were three main models of the BAR, the M1918, the M1918A1 and the M1918A2. The M1918 was the basic hand-held model, the M1918A1 had a bipod and the M1918A2 retained the bipod and had two rates of automatic fire and no semi-automatic feature. Licence built models were produced by FN in Belgium in the 1930s and others were made in Poland and Sweden. Some American police forces still use a commercial model, the 'Monitor', and the BAR is still in army use in Greece, Costa Rica, Guatemala, Indondesia, Mexico, Norway and the Philippines.

The Browning Model M1918A2 automatic rifle.

.30in M1903 Rifle Series United States

Data: M1903A1
Calibre: .30in (7.62mm)
Length: 109.7cm
Length of barrel: 61cm
Weight: 3.95kg
Mag capacity: 5 rounds

Muzzle velocity: 823m/s
Max effective range: 600m

Despite its age, the M1903 series of rifles (the M1903, M1903A1, M1903A3 and M1903A4) are still to be encountered in areas of American influence. Often known as the Springfield, the M1903 range remained in use throughout World War II and the M1903A3 continued to be produced until 1943. The M1903A4 was fitted with a telescopic sight. Although the M1903 has now been almost universally taken out of front-line service it is still used as a weapon by local militia and self defence

The .30in M1903 rifle complete with bayonet.

units in all parts of the world. The Mauser action used is sturdy and well made and the Springfield is likely to remain in use for years to come. The series is favoured for match shooting.

Special Purpose Individual Weapon United States

Development of the SPIW started in the 1950s and a variety of prototypes have been built by a number of companies and government establishments. Among the companies have been Harrington and Richardson, Aircraft Armaments Incorporated and Olin-Winchester. To date none of the weapons has

been placed in production. Currently a number of companies and establishments in the United States are working on a weapon to replace the current M16 rifle; the programme is known as the Future Rifle System.

Squad Automatic Weapon System United States

In the early 1970s, the United States Army Weapons Command held a competition for a weapon which would meet the Army's requirement for a future Squad Automatic Weapon System (SAWS). After the initial trials three weapons remained, the Maremont Corporation XM233, the Philco-Ford XM234 and the Rodman Laboratories (Rock Island) XM235, all of which fired a 6mm round designated the XM732 which had been developed by Frankford Arsenal. In 1975, the Department of Defense decided that the weapons must fire a 5.56mm round

but the whole project was subsequently shelved to await the outcome of the NATO Small Arms Trials. Other weapons originally considered were the Maremont Universal machine gun (details of which were given in the first edition of *Infantry Weapons of the World*), the German HK21, the Colt CMG-2 and the Belgian 5.56mm Minimi, the latter being the best of the foreign weapons tested according to one report.

The XM233 SAWS contender.

5.56mm Hughes Lockless Light Machine Gun

United States

Calibre: 5.56mm
Length: 109.2cm
Weight: 8.165kg (with mag containing 200 rounds)
Mag capacity: 200 rounds
Range: 600m
Rate of fire: 420rpm

The 5.56mm Lockless Light Machine Gun (LLMG) is an advanced automatic weapon which, coupled with its plastic cased ammunition, represents a major advance in the field of small arms. Sponsored initially by the Advanced Research Projects Agency and now under contract to the United States Army Armament Command, the Hughes developed weapon is based on the Lockless principle of a sliding sleeve mechanism. This eliminates the need for the primary sealing function normally provided by the standard metallic cartridge case, thus the use of lighter and more compact plastic cased ammunition is feasible and has been demonstrated.

The weapon is provided with a detachable bipod and is gas-operated. The expendable magazine can be loaded and stored indefinitely and its capacity is six times that of any assault weapon and double that of all existing light machine guns.

The Hughes designed, plastic cased, fully tele-scoped rectangular cartridge uses a 5.56mm pro-jectile weighing 68gr, as compared with the standard 55gr projectile. Test firings have already demonstrated both superior ballistics and an excellent growth potential. The round has a m/v of 914m/s. The weapon is still being developed and is not yet in production.

The Hughes 5.56mm Lockless LMG.

Lockless Rifle/Machine Gun

United States

Calibre: 5.56mm
Length: 101.6cm (overall)
74.87cm (stock folded)
Length of barrel: 55.8cm
Weight: 4.44kg (with mag)
Mag capacity: 64 rounds
Muzzle velocity: 944m/s
Effective range: 600m
Rate of fire: 420rpm

The Lockless Rifle/Machine Gun (LRMG) has been developed by the Ordnance Division of the Hughes Company of Culver City, California. The LRMG is the result of Hughes' continued work on a prototype funded under the Advanced Research Projects Agency. The weapon has a number of interesting features and is based on the 'lockless' principle of a sliding sleeve mechanism.

It fires a new 5.56mm 68gr fully-telescoped rectangular cartridge with a case of plastic construc-tion. The LRMG is gas-operated and the firer can select either single shots or full automatic fire. A detachable bipod is provided and the barrel can be quickly changed. According to Hughes it takes only three seconds to change the magazine.

5.56mm Colt CMG-2 Machine Gun

United States

Calibre: 5.56mm
Length: 106.5cm
Weight: 5.9kg (guns only)
7.31kg (complete with drum and bipod)
Range: 800m with 68gr bullet
600m with 55gr bullet
Muzzle velocity: 991m/s, or 884m/s with 68gr bullet
Rate of fire: 650rpm (cyclic)
120rpm (sustained)

The Colt 5.56mm CMG-2 machine gun has been developed to the prototype stage by the Military Arms Division of Colt Industries who also make the current M16A1 Rifle. The weapon is at present under evaluation and has not yet been placed in production.

It is gas-operated and its method of locking is of the rotating bolt type. It is belt fed from a 150-round drum which is underneath the weapon and the barrel can be quickly changed. A carrying handle is provided over the barrel. The fore sight is of the fixed post type and the rear sight is of the aperture type.

Although the CMG-2 can fire the standard 5.56mm 55gr M193 cartridge a more powerful cartridge 68gr has been developed. This has a lower muzzle velocity but a longer range.

Note — the Colt CMG-1 5.56mm system which comprised a rifle, LMG gun MMG and an armoured vehicle MG, was not developed beyond the prototype stage.

7.62mm M60 GPMG

United States

Calibre: 7.62mm
Length: 110cm
Length of barrel: 56cm
Weight: 10.48kg
Type of feed: link belt
Muzzle velocity: 860m/s
Max effective range: 800m (with bipod)
1,800m (with tripod)
Rate of fire: 550rpm (cyclic)
200rpm (auto)

The concept of the General Purpose Machine Gun in the United States was accelerated during World War II by confrontation with the German MG34 and MG42. An American GPMG was designed along the lines of the MG42 in a series of guns in the series T44, T52 and T161. The T161 became the M60 and the design incorporates a modified MG42 feed with

the operating mechanism of the German FG42. The prime producer of the M60 has been the Maremont Manufacturing Co of Saco in Maine, and large numbers have been produced to equip all arms of the US forces. Also the M60 is rather on the heavy side for use as a squad weapon. Mounted on the M122 tripod, the M60 has limitations on sustained fire. Vehicle mounting is the M4 pedestal mount. Basically, the M60 is gas-operated and can fire automatic only. A bipod is fitted as standard and is also used for barrel changing. As well as being the standard American GPMG, the M60 is also used by Australia and Taiwan, and was widely issued to many SE Asian countries.

The M60C and M60D are conversions of the basic M60 for use on helicopters.

The standard M60 machine gun on a bipod.

.30in Browning M1919A6 Machine Gun   United States

Calibre: .30in (7.62mm)
Length: 134.6cm (overall)
Length of barrel: 61cm
Weight: 14.77kg (complete)
Type of feed: 250-round belt
Muzzle velocity: 860m/s
Max effective range: 1,000m
Rate of fire: 400-550rpm (cyclic)
120rpm (auto)

At the beginning of World War II the US Army found itself without an LMG and took steps to procure one by adapting the M1919A4. By the addition of a

bipod, butt stock and pistol grip a rather heavy but serviceable light machine gun was produced and it was produced in some numbers as the M1919A6. After 1945, the M1919A6 was gradually withdrawn from use, despite a brief respite during the Korean War, and was sold or given to many friendly nations. Today, it would appear that it use is now confined to the armies of Taiwan, Turkey and Pakistan, but it is no doubt held as a reserve weapon by many other countries.

The .30in Browning M1919A6 machine gun.

.30in Browning M1919A4 Machine Gun   United States

Calibre: .30in (7.62mm)
Length: 104.4cm
Length of barrel: 61cm
Weight: 14.1kg (gun)
6.36kg (M2 tripod)
Type of feed: 250-round belt
Muzzle velocity: 860m/s
Max effective range: 1,000m
Rate of fire: 400-550rpm (cyclic)
120rpm (practical)

The M1919A4 is an air-cooled version of the earlier M1917 water-cooled machine gun which apparently is no longer in service anywhere. The M1919A4 was produced in large numbers during

World War II and has proved itself to be a reliable weapon. As a result it is still likely to be found on a wide range of tripods. AA-mountings and vehicle and AFV pintles. One of the more common mountings is the Tripod M2. As well as remaining in widespread use with the US forces, the M1919A4 is in service with the following countries:
Canada (rechambered for the NATO cartridge as the 7.62mm Machine Gun C1), Taiwan, Denmark (.30in M52-1), Dominica, Greece, Guatemala, Haiti, Israel, Iran, Italy, South Korea, Liberia, Mexico, Panama, Spain, Vietnam, Turkey.

The .30in Browning M1919A4 machine gun on a tripod.

.5in Browning M2 Machine Gun

United States

Data: M2HB
Calibre: .5in (12.7mm)
Length: 165.3cm (overall)
Length of barrel: 114.3cm
Weight: 37.8kg
Type of feed: 110-round linked belts
Muzzle velocity: 893m/s
Max effective range: 1,000m
Rate of fire: 450-575rpm (cyclic)

The Browning family of .5in machine guns was initiated just after World War I and since then the basic mechanism and receiver has remained virtually unchanged. The type of barrel and cooling method have been changed from model to model but today the version most likely to be encountered is the M2HB (HB-heavy barrel). This version has an air-cooled barrel and it can be mounted on a variety of vehicle pintles or on the M3 tripod or M63 anti-

The .50in Browning machine gun on ring mount.

aircraft mounting. The M2 is a powerful weapon that has not lost its place in modern armouries, despite its age. The round fired by the M2 is useful against light armour and low-flying aircraft and helicopters and as an anti-personnel projectile it is almost unrivalled. However, the size and weight of the M2 mean that it is more likely to be used from a vehicle pintle than a ground mounting. More Browning .5in machine guns. have been made than any other American machine gun.

Other users:

Argentina, Australia, Austria, Belgium, Canada, Chile, Denmark (m/50), France, Haiti, Iran, Israel, Italy, Japan, South Korea, Liberia, Morocco, Netherlands, Norway, Pakistan, Spain, Taiwan, Turkey.

Viper Light Anti-Tank Weapon

United States

Weight: 3.18kg
Length: 68.5cm (carrying)
111.7cm (ready to fire)

The Viper light anti-tank weapon has been developed by the Pomona Division of General Dynamics as the successor to the current M66 light anti-tank weapon. The Viper consists of a free-flight, in-tube burning rocket which is packaged and sealed in an expendable launcher that also serves as a storage container. The rocket is fin-stabilised and has a shaped charged warhead which will defeat the armour of any Soviet tank currently in service, it is also lethal against other battlefield targets such as trucks. The exact range of the Viper has not been revealed but it is thought to be in excess of 400m.

The weapon is simple to operate as all the soldier has to do is to extend the launch tube (which automatically deploys the front sight), pull open the

shoulder stop, erect the rear sight, aim, arm and fire. Once the weapon has been fired the launcher is discarded. Development of the Viper is now complete and it is expected that it will enter service with the United States Army in 1980.

CARRY MODE

ROCKET

LAUNCHER

FIRING MECHANISM

CARRYING STRAP

READY-TO-FIRE MODE

AFT END CAP

LAUNCHER ASSY

REAR SIGHT

FIRING MECHANISM ASSY

FORWARD SIGHT

ROCKET

SABOT

SHOULDER STOP

TUBE EXTENSION LOCK ASSY

FORWARD END CAP

66mm M72A1 and M72A2 Rocket Launcher United States

Calibre: 66mm
Length: 89.3cm (launcher-extended)
65.5cm (launcher closed)
50.8cm (rocket)
Weight: 2.37kg (complete)
1kg (rocket)
Muzzle velocity: 145m/s
Max effective range: 300m
Armour penetration: 30.5cm steel plate

Designed as a one-man rocket launcher for anti-tank use, the M72 has been replaced in service by the M72A1 and M72A2 (the two are identical except that the M72A2 has an increased penetration capability). When carried, the smooth-bore launcher tube is closed, and in this form is water-proof. In action, the end covers are opened, which is done by removing safety pins, and the inner tube is telescoped outwards and this cocks the firing mechanism. The launcher tube is then held over the shoulder, aimed by the simple sights and fired by pressing the trigger button. The rocket motor is fully burnt by the time it leaves the launcher but this also leaves a large 'danger' area behind the firer. Once used the launcher tube is discarded. The 66mm rocket has now become a standard infantry anti-tank weapon in many armies. The M71A1 and M71A2 are 35mm sub-calibre training devices. The model is also built in Norway by Raufoss for issue to NATO forces.

The 66mm M72 anti-tank rocket.

90mm M67 Recoilless Rifle   United States

Calibre: 90mm
Length: 134.6cm
Weight: 15.87kg
Range: 450m
Crew: 1-2

The M67 is an air-cooled portable anti-tank weapon and can be fired from the prone position or the shoulder. It is being replaced in the United States Army by the Dragon ATGW.

It consists of a front mounting bracket group, cable assembly, face shield group, breech and hinge mechanism group, rear mounting bracket group and

the rifled tube itself. It is fitted with a M103 telescope which has a magnification of ×3 and a 10° field of view.

It fires a fin-stabilised HEAT round weighing 3.1kg which has a m/v of 213m/s. An anti-personnel round has also been developed.

The 90mm M67 recoilless rifle.

57mm M18 Recoilless Rifle   United States

Calibre: 57mm
Length: 156.2cm
Length of barrel: 122cm
Weight: 18.2kg
Range: 400m (effective)
4.000m (max)
Crew: 1-2

There are three basic models of this weapon, the M18, M18A1, and the T15E16. These can be fired from the ground, shoulder or from a M74 or M1917A2 mount. The complete weapon consists of the barrel group, breech mechanism group, a firing cable group, trigger mechanism group, bipod assembly and an extendable handle assembly.

The M18 and M18A1 have their chamber and breechblock handles located in different positions. The M18 has its one the left and the M18A1 is on the right. The major difference between the M18A1 and the T15E16 is in the linkage between the trigger mechanism group and the breech mechanism group. The following types of ammunition are available: HE (m/v 365m/s), HEAT (m/v 365m/s), canister, WP

(m/v 365m/s) and TP. Its effective range in the anti-tank role is approx 400m and its maximum range, at 39° elevation, with a HEAT round is 4,000m. It is provided with an M86F (M86C) telescope which has a 7° field of view and a magnification of ×2.8.

The M18 is built in Communist China under the designation Type 36.

A 57mm M18 recoilless rifle being used by the Norwegian Army.

3.5in M20 Rocket Launcher

United States

Calibre: 3.5in (88.9mm)
Length: 154.9cm (launcher)
Weight: 4.04kg (rocket)
.87kg (rocket warhead)
5.5kg (launcher)
Muzzle velocity: 97 to 147m/s
Range: 110m (max effective anti-tank)
1,200m (max)
Rate of fire: 6rpm

The M20 was developed from the earlier 2.36in M9A1 rocket launcher at the time of the Korean War and since that time it has kept its place as one of the main anti-tank weapons of many armies. The M20, often known as the 'Bazooka', is a simple rocket launcher firing a hollow-charge rocket projectile to relatively short ranges. It requires a two-man team. When carried, the long tube is folded into two for easier handling. In action a rocket is loaded into the open breech and two wires are secured to two electrical terminals. When the trigger is pulled a small electrical current ignites the rocket motor

The 3.5in M20 rocket launcher.

which projects the rocket forward, leaving a large and dangerous flame area behind the projector. Although the M20 and its developments the M20A1, M20A1B1 and M20AB2, are no longer in front-line service with the US forces, they remain in use with many other armies but they are gradually being replaced. China continues to use a copy known as the Type 51, and many smaller countries make their own ammunition, Spain (the firm of Instalaza SA) being an example.

Other users:

Argentina, China, Denmark (89mm RK M/51), Dominica, France (LRAC M20), Greece, Guatemala, India, Iran, Italy, Japan, South Korea, Liberia, Malaysia, Morocco, Norway, Pakistan, Panama, Portugal, Spain (88.9mm Model 65 Lanzagranadas), Turkey, Vietnam.

40mm M79 Grenade Launcher
United States

Calibre: 40mm
Length: 73.7cm
Length of barrel: 35.6cm
Weight: 2.95kg (loaded)
2.72kg (empty)
.227kg (grenade)
Muzzle velocity: 76m/s
Range: 150m (max effective point target)
400m (approx max)

The M79 is a break-open single-shot weapon designed to be fired from the shoulder. It is breech-loaded and fires a 40mm metal cartridge case with an internal primer. The ammunition available covers a wide range from smoke to HE and riot rounds, and these rounds can be fired to a range in excess of that obtainable from normal rifle grenades with a reasonable degree of accuracy. The rear sights on the M79 are near the muzzle as the low m/v requires high elevation angles to reach maximum ranges. Although it is still in widespread use with the American forces, the M79 is gradually being replaced by the smaller and lighter M203 launcher which can be fitted on to the M16 rifle.

The 40mm M79 Grenade Launcher.

40mm XM174 Automatic Grenade Launcher
United States

Calibre: 40mm
Length: 71.12cm
Weight: 11.75kg (loaded less pintle)
.227kg (grenade)
Mag capacity: 12 rounds
Muzzle velocity: 76m/s (normal round)
Range: 400m (max normal round)
1,000m (max new round)

The success of the M79 grenade launcher has led to the normal infantry squad having a greatly increased fire power against area targets. Since the M79 and the M203 are both only single-shot weapons, a demand for an automatic launcher arose. The result is the XM174 Automatic Grenade Launcher, produced by the Aerojet Ordnance and Manufacturing Co of Downey, California. This weapon uses a conventional blow-back mechanism which can be selected for automatic or semi-automatic fire, and grenades are held in a twelve-round magazine on the LHS of the receiver. The XM174 is designed primarily for use from vehicles, fitted on a pintle, but it can also be fitted to the M122 tripod. At present the range of the XM174 is limited to the current grenades in service but a new series of grenades is under development which will have a range of up to 1,000m. At the time of writing

The 40mm automatic grenade launcher XM174 without tripod.

the latest version is the XM174E3 under extended trials by the US Marine Corps.

60mm M224 Lightweight Company Mortar United States

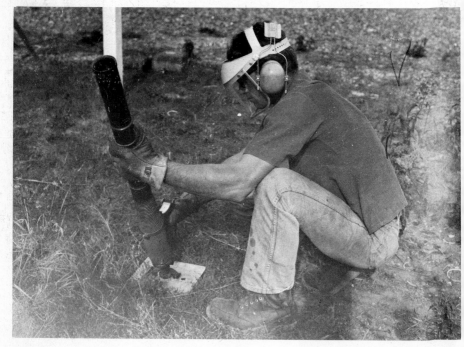

The 60mm M224 Lightweight Company Mortar was developed from December 1970 as the XM224 to replace the current 81mm mortar in rifle companies of infantry, airmobile infantry and airborne infantry. Development of the M224 has now been completed and the Fiscal Year 1978 request was for a total of 190 mortars at a cost of $3.4million with the Fiscal Year 1979 request being for a further 2,098 mortars at a cost of $14.2million. Production of the mortar is undertaken at Watervliet Arsenal, New York.

The circular baseplate is an aluminium forging and a lightweight rectangular baseplate has also been developed. Total weight of the M224, ie baseplate,

barrel, bipod and sight is only 20.4kg. The mortar can be fired by the conventional gravity method or by a firing pin. The M64 sight used with the mortar weighs 1.1kg.

The mortar bomb is provided with a multi-option fuse which allows the crew to select airburst, near-surface burst, direct action or delayed action.

The Automated Systems Division of RCA have developed a new lightweight laser rangefinder known as the AN/GVS-5 for use with the M224 mortar. This weighs only 2kg and can range up to 10,000m with an accuracy of ±10m.

60mm M19 Mortar United States

Calibre: 60mm
Length: 81.9cm (overall)
Weight: 20.545kg (complete)
1.363kg (M49A2 bomb)
Elevation: +40° to +85° (M5 Mount)
Range: 1,790m (M49A2 max)
Rate of fire: 30rpm (max)
18rpm (sustained)

The M19 was originally issued with a simple base plate, the M1, and no tripod. With the demise of the

earlier 60mm Mortar M2, however, the M19 was fitted with the M5 tripod and remained in use for some years. It has now been largely replaced in front-line service with the American forces but it is still in widespread use in SE Asia and in many South American countries as is the earlier M2. China uses a copy of the M2 in the Type 31.

The 60mm M19 light mortar.

7.62mm Type 50 Sub-Machine Gun Vietnam

Calibre: 7.62mm
Length: 75.6cm (stock extended)
65cm (stock retracted)
Length of barrel: 26.7cm
Weight: 4.5kg (approx)
Mag capacity: 35 rounds
Muzzle velocity: 500m/s

Range: 200m
Rate of fire: 900rpm (cyclic)

This North Vietnamese weapon is a 'local' variation of the Chinese Type 50 sub-machine gun which is itself a copy of the Soviet PPSh-41. In addition to this Type 50 basis this weapon features the pistol

20

grip and front sight of the Chinese Type 56 assault rifle while the wire stock is a copy of that used on the French MAT 49. This amalgam was produced in some numbers but not surprisingly, the finish of many is rough and variations on the above dimensions can be expected.

Type 50 SMG complete with pouch with three magazines.

7.62mm M57 and 9mm M70(d) Pistols   Yugoslavia

	M57	M70(d)
Calibre:	7.62mm	9mm
Length:	20cm	20cm
Length of barrel:	11.6cm	11.6cm
Weight (empty):	0.9kg	0.9kg
Mag capacity:	9 rounds	9 rounds
Muzzle velocity:	450m/s	330m/s

The M57 is basically the Russian Tokarev TT-33 built by Zavodi Crevena Zastava in Yugoslavia and can be distinguished from the Russian weapon by the star type emblem on the grip. Its method of operation is identical to the Russian TT-33. The Model M70(d) is the M57 built to fire the 9mm × 19mm Parabellum cartridge and is identical to the earlier weapon except that it has six-groove rifling instead of four-groove.

7.62mm M70 and 9mm M70(k) Pistols   Yugoslavia

	M70	M70(k)
Calibre:	7.62mm	9mm
Length:	20cm	20cm
Length of barrel:	9.4cm	9.4cm
Weight empty:	0.74kg	0.72kg
Mag capacity:	8 rounds	8 rounds
Muzzle velocity:	300m/s	260m/s

These two pistols are further developments of the earlier M57 (7.62mm) and M70(d) (9mm Parabellum) weapons but have shorter barrels, are lighter and their magazines hold eight rather than nine rounds of ammunition. As a result of these and other improvements the weapons are easier to handle and are more accurate.

7.62mm M56 Sub-Machine Gun   Yugoslavia

Calibre: 7.62mm
Length: 104cm (with bayonet)
86.5cm (stock extended)
64cm (stock folded)
Length of barrel: 25cm
Weight: 3.73kg (loaded mag)
3.38kg (empty mag)
3.06kg (without mag)
Mag capacity: 32 rounds
Range: 200m (semi-auto)
100m (auto)
Rate of fire: 570/620rpm (cyclic)
180rmp (auto)
30rpm (semi-auto)

The M56 was developed to replace the earlier M49 SMG. In appearance the M56 is similar to both the Soviet PPS M1943 SMG and the German MP40. The M56 is blowback operated and is capable of both full automatic and semi-automatic fire. The M56 fires the same 7.62mm × 25mm cartridge with a m/v of 500m/s as the earlier M49. It is provided with a folding stock and a bayonet can be fitted if required. The front sight is of the hooded post type and the rear sight is of the flip type set for 100 and 200m.

7.62mm M49 Sub-Machine Gun   Yugoslavia

Calibre: 7.62mm
Length: 87.4cm
Length of barrel: 27.3cm
Weight: 4.66kg (loaded mag)
4.25kg (empty mag)
3.96kg (without mag)
Mag capacity: 35 rounds
Range: 200m (semi-auto)
100m (auto)
Rate of fire: 700rpm (cyclic)
120/150rpm (auto)
30/40rpm (semi-auto)

The M49 is a Yugoslav weapon developed from the Soviet PPSh-41 which was used in large numbers by Yugoslavia. The main differences lay in the bolt, buffer assembly and the barrel casing. The M49 has circular holes in the casing rather than the long slots which are found on the Soviet weapon. Also, the Yugoslav weapon has only a 35-round magazine although it will accept a Soviet PPSh-41 magazine. The M49 is blowback operated and can be used either full automatic or semi-automatic. Its front sight is of the blade post type and its rearsights are of the flip type graduated for 100 and 200m. It fires the 7.62mm × 25mm cartridge with a m/v of 500m/s or the 7.63mm Mauser cartridge.

7.62mm M64A (or Model 70) Assault Rifle   Yugoslavia

The Yugoslav 7.62mm M64B (or Model 70A) assault rifle. This has a folding stock, grenade launching sight and a compensator screwed on to the barrel.

Calibre: 7.62mm
Length: 115.7cm (with bayonet)
95.7cm (without)
Length of barrel: 41.5cm
Weight: 4.19kg (with loaded aluminium mag)
4.25kg (with loaded late steel mag)
4.35kg (with loaded early steel mag)
3.69kg (with empty aluminium mag)
3.75kg (with empty late steel mag)
3.85kg (with empty early steel mag)
3.46kg (without mag)
Mag capacity: 20 or 30 rounds
Range: 400m
Rate of fire: 600rpm (cyclic)
40/120rpm (practical)

There are three models of this weapon built in Yugoslavia. The first of these is the M64 which has a barrel 100mm longer than that of the M64A, this is therefore referred to as an automatic rifle rather than an assault rifle. All are based on the Soviet AK assault rifle. The second model is the M64A which more recently has become known as the Model 70 assault rifle; this has a fixed wooden stock. The third model is the M64B which recently has become known as the Model 70A; this has a folding stock. These weapons have a permanently attached spigot type grenade launcher. When the grenade sight is raised it cuts off the supply to the gas cylinder. It is reported that the M64, when fitted with a bipod, is known as the M72 LMG.

7.62mm M59/66 Rifle   Yugoslavia

Calibre: 7.62mm
Length: 132cm (with bayonet)
125.5cm (without)
Length of barrel: 52cm
Weight: 4.2kg (loaded)
4.03kg (with empty mag)
Mag capacity: 10 rounds
Range: 400m
Rate of fire: 30rpm

The first M59 was a direct copy of the Soviet SKS (Simonov) rifle. The M59/66 was a later development by the Yugoslavs. The main differences are that it has a longer knife type bayonet and a permanently attached spigot type grenade launcher. When the grenade sight is not required it is folded flat behind the foresight. The M59/66 fires the 7.62mm × 39mm cartridge with a m/v of 735m/s.

The M59/66 can fire the following types of rifle grenades, as can the M48 rifle:
F-1/N60: Weight .632kg, range 240m.
PGN 60: Weight .58kg, range 100m (anti-tank).
YugAT: Weight .602kg, range 150m (anti-tank).
YugAPers: Weight .52kg, range 400m (anti-personnel).

7.62mm M65A and M65B Light Machine Gun Yugoslavia

Calibre: 7.62mm
Length: 109.5cm
Length of barrel: 47cm
Weight: 5.45kg
Mag capacity: 30 rounds
Range: 600m
Rate of fire: 600rpm (cyclic)
120rpm (auto-M65B)
80rpm (auto-M65A)
40rpm (semi-auto)

This weapon is based on the Yugoslav assault rifle M64A which in turn is based on the Soviet AK

weapon. The M65A has a fixed barrel whilst the M65B has a quick-change barrel. Both weapons are gas-operated with a selective fire facility, fire the 7.62mm × 39mm cartridge with a m/v of 732m/s and have a cone shaped flash hider attached to their muzzles. The fore sight is of the cylindrical post type and the rear sight is of the leaf notch type. Yugoslavia also uses the German World War II MG42 (qv) machine gun which they call the M53 SARAC.

RB-57 Anti-Tank Grenade Launcher Yugoslavia

Calibre: 90mm (launcher)
44mm (tube)
Weight of launcher: 8.35kg
Length of tube: 96cm
Range: 1,200m (max)
400m (effective stationary target)
200m (effective moving target)
Rate of fire: 4rpm
Crew: 2 men

The RB-57 anti-tank grenade launcher.

After World War II the Yugoslavs developed a number of anti-tank launchers. The first model was called the M49 (or RB-49) and fired a HEAT round. It was provided with a folding bipod, shoulder rest and sling but did not go into service. One unusual feature of the M49 was that it had a six-round magazine for ignition cartridges.

The current Yugoslav anti-tank grenade launcher is the M57 (or RB-57) as it is often called. Late models are known as the M57A (or RB-57A) and M57A2 (or RB-57A2). Each fires a HEAT round weighing 2.44kg and 1.104m in length, m/v is 145m/s, the projectile itself is 75.7cm in length and weighs 1.84kg. It will penetrate 270mm of armour.

The M57 is provided with conventional sights for 100, 200, 300 and 400m; in addition there is an emergency sight for 200m. An optical sight is also available, sighted to 400m. The sight is on the LHS with the loader to the right. A bipod is provided.

The primers for the projectile are located in the sidewall of the tailboom with a right angle flash channel leading to the propellent. The spring loaded striker, which is at the bottom of the launcher tube, is actuated by a double action trigger mechanism.

60mm M57 Light Mortar

Yugoslavia

Calibre: 60.75mm
Length of barrel: 70.8cm
Weight: 19.7kg (total)
5.5kg (barrel)
4.5kg (bipod)
8.85kg (baseplate)
Elevation: +45° to +83°
Traverse: 7°
Range: 74m (min)
1,690m (max)
Rate of fire: 25-30rpm (max)
Crew: 2

Essentially a Yugoslav model of the American 60mm mortar M2, the M57 fires a bomb weighing 1.35kg at a m/v of 159m/s. Types of bomb available include

HE, smoke and illuminating. The crew normally consists of two men, the aimer on the left and the loader on the right.

The Yugoslavs also have a 50mm light mortar called the M8 which is similar to the British 2in mortar. Basic data is as follows: calibre 50mm, weight 7.3kg, weight of bomb .92kg, max range 480m and min range 135m.

Bibliography

There are many excellent publications on small arms, listed below are the standard reference books on the subject. Without doubt *Jane's Infantry Weapons* is the most authoritative book on infantry weapons. The first edition was edited by the late Major F. W. A. Hobart, one of the world's leading experts on small-arms design and development. Other publications include:

Book of Pistols; W. H. B. Smith and J. E. Smith (Arms and Armour Press, London)
Book of Rifles; W. H. B. Smith and J. E. Smith (Arms and Armour Press, London)
Jane's Infantry Weapons, 1975; Major F. W. A. Hobart (Macdonald Jane's of London)
Jane's Infantry Weapons, 1976, 1977 and 1978; D. H. Archer (Macdonald Jane's of London)
Leichte Infanteriewaffen; Nikolaus Krivinyi (Verlag Carl Uebereuter, Vienna)
Military Small Arms of the 20th Century; I. Hogg and John Weeks (Arms and Armour Press, London)
Pictorial History of the Machine Gun; Major F. W. A. Hobart (Ian Allan, London)
Pictorial History of the Rifle; G. W. P. Swenson (Ian Allan, London)
Pictorial History of the Sub-Machine Gun; Major F. W. A. Hobart (Ian Allan, London)
Small Arms of the World; (Arms and Armour Press, London)

Photo Credits

The photographs used to illustrate this book have been received from many governments, companies and individuals all over the world. Special thanks are due to the staff of the Pattern Room at The Royal Small Arms Factory at Enfield Lock, Middlesex, for their assistance in taking many of the photographs used in this book. The sources of photographs, where known, are listed below:

Aerojet Ordnance and Manufacturing Company 126(T)
AIC (USA) 9
Argentine Ministry of Defence 7(T)
Austrian Army 11(T), 52
Beretta (Italy) 70, 71, 72, 73, 74, 75(T&C)
Breda (Italy) 75
Carl Walther 40, 41, 42(T), 46(T)
CETME (Spain) 96, 97
Christopher F. Foss 55
Colt Fire Arms Inc (USA) 113(T&C)
ECIA (Spain) 98, 99(T)
FFV (Sweden) 101(B), 102(T)
Finnish Army 29, 30, 32(B)
FN of Herstal (Belgium) 11(B), 12(B), 14, 15, 16(T)
French Army (ECPA) 33, 35(T), 36
General Dynamics (USA) 122(T)
German Army 39(B)
GIAT (France) 34(B)

Heckler and Koch (Germany) 42(B), 43, 44(B), 45, 47, 48, 49, 50(T&C), 51(B), 56(T)
Hotchkiss-Brandt (France) 37, 38, 39(T)
Hughes Company (USA) 118
IMI (Israel) 67, 68, 69(T)
Interdynamic AB (Sweden) 100
Maremont Corp (USA) 117(B)
MBB (Germany) 54(B)
Ministry of Defence 63(B)
Norwegian Army 124(T)
Parker-Hale (Great Britain) 60(B)
Rheinmetall Company (Germany) 58(T&B)
Steyr-Daimler-Puch (Austria) 10
Sturm, Ruger and Co (USA) 110
Tampella (Israel) 69
Terry Gander 7(B), 8, 12(T), 13, 16(C&B), 17, 18, 19, 20, 21, 22, 23, 24, 25, 26, 27, 28, 34(T), 35(B), 44(T), 46(B), 50(B), 51(T), 56(B), 57, 59, 60(T), 61, 62, 63(T), 64, 65(B), 66, 77, 79, 80, 81, 82, 83, 84, 85(B), 86, 87, 88, 89, 90, 92, 93, 94, 95, 99(B), 101(T), 102(B), 106(T), 107, 108, 109, 111(C&B), 112, 113(B), 114, 115, 116, 117(T), 120, 122(B), 125, 128, 129, 130
United States Army 123, 126(B), 127
United States Marine Corps 114(B)
Valmet (Finland) 31, 32(T)

Index

Other Series Titles

Air Forces of the World
Civil Aircraft of the World
Helicopters of the World
Military Aircraft of the World
Missiles of the World
World Civil Aircraft Since 1945
World Military Aircraft Since 1945
Armoured Fighting Vehicles of the World
Artillery of the World
Military Vehicles of the World
Warships of the World — 1 Major Classes
Warships of the World — 2 Escort Vessels
Police of the World

In Preparation

Police Vehicles of the World
Emergency Service Vehicles of the UK
World Armoured Fighting Vehicles Since 1945
Armies of the World
World Military Aircraft 1918-1939
Warships of the World — 3 Submarines and Fast
  Attack Craft